NATIONAL GEOGRAPHIC
KiDS

CAN'T GET ENOUGH

SHARK
Stuff

FUN FACTS, AWESOME INFO, COOL GAMES, SILLY JOKES, AND MORE!

KELLY HARGRAVE AND ANDREA SILEN

NATIONAL GEOGRAPHIC
WASHINGTON, D.C.

TABLE OF
CONTENTS

HOORAY FOR SHARKS!

WHOOSH! Sharks dip and dive across the ocean. Some zip through rivers, lakes, and bays. Others lurk in underwater caves. The world's waters are filled with these fantastic fish.

Sharks come in all shapes and sizes, with hundreds of different species featuring jaw-dropping senses and skills. These top predators have been around for a long, long time: more than 400 million years! Sharks date back to way before the dinosaurs—so far back, they're even older than trees!

This book is your number one source for shark fun. Inside, you'll find bite-size shark facts, quizzes to test your shark smarts, and plenty of jokes. Chomp on amazing stats about sharks, from the speeds they can swim to the sizes they can reach. Sink your teeth into some fun shark games, such as matching challenges and word scrambles. Get your fins dirty with wild experiments that reveal surprising shark secrets and powers. Read stories from shark experts, dig into stories about shark fossils, and go swimming with tiger sharks, thresher sharks, oceanic whitetip sharks, and more.

So get ready—it's time to dive in!

CATCH AND MATCH

These jaw-dropping shark terms will help you be a shark pro in no time! Catch a word and see if you can match it with the correct definition. Write your answers (numbered 1–20) on a separate piece of paper. Then compare them to the answer key at the bottom of page 9.

1 CAMOUFLAGE

2 CARTILAGE

3 DERMAL DENTICLES

4 GILLS

5 FOSSIL

6 HABITAT

7 LATERAL LINES

8 PORE

9 SPECIES

10 VERTEBRAE

11 BUOYANCY

12 MOLECULES

13 SEDIMENT

14 ACIDIC

15 BIO-LUMINESCENCE

16 BIO-FLUORESCENCE

17 NICTITATING MEMBRANE

18 BINOCULAR VISION

19 BOTTOM DWELLER

20 EMIT

A — The place where an animal or plant naturally lives

B — V-shaped, toothlike scales on shark skin

C — When two eyes focus on an object to create a single image

D — A small hole

E — Sensors on a shark's body that run in a line all the way from its snout to its tail

F — A pattern or color that covers a shark's body, making it difficult to spot

G — The preserved body part, track, or trace of an ancient animal or plant

H — A group of similar living things

I — All the pieces of cartilage that make up a shark's spine

J — The ability to float in water or liquid

K — When a living thing absorbs blue light and sends the light back out as a different color

L — The smallest elements that make up us and our surroundings

M — When freshwater contains too many harsh chemicals and is no longer safe

N — When living things create light within their bodies

O — A living thing that lives or feeds at the bottom level of a body of water

P — A stretchy material found in the bodies of animals

Q — A white or see-through layer of skin that acts as an inner eyelid on some animals

R — Natural material broken down and carried by wind, water, or ice

S — To give off something, especially light or gas

T — Vertical slits near the front of the shark that allow it to breathe

ANSWERS: 1. F, 2. P, 3. B, 4. T, 5. G, 6. A, 7. E, 8. D, 9. H, 10. I, 11. J, 12. L, 13. R, 14. M, 15. N, 16. K, 17. G, 18. C, 19. O, 20. S

9

FISH FUNNIES

Q Which sharks always hit the snooze button on their alarms?

A Sleeper sharks.

Q What do sharks use for money?

A Sand dollars.

Q What's on a shark's playlist?

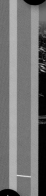

A Their top tunas.

TONGUE TWISTER

SAY THIS FAST THREE TIMES:
Whale sharks whistle while whooshing by.

Q What do sharks say when they sneeze?

A "Ah-chew!"

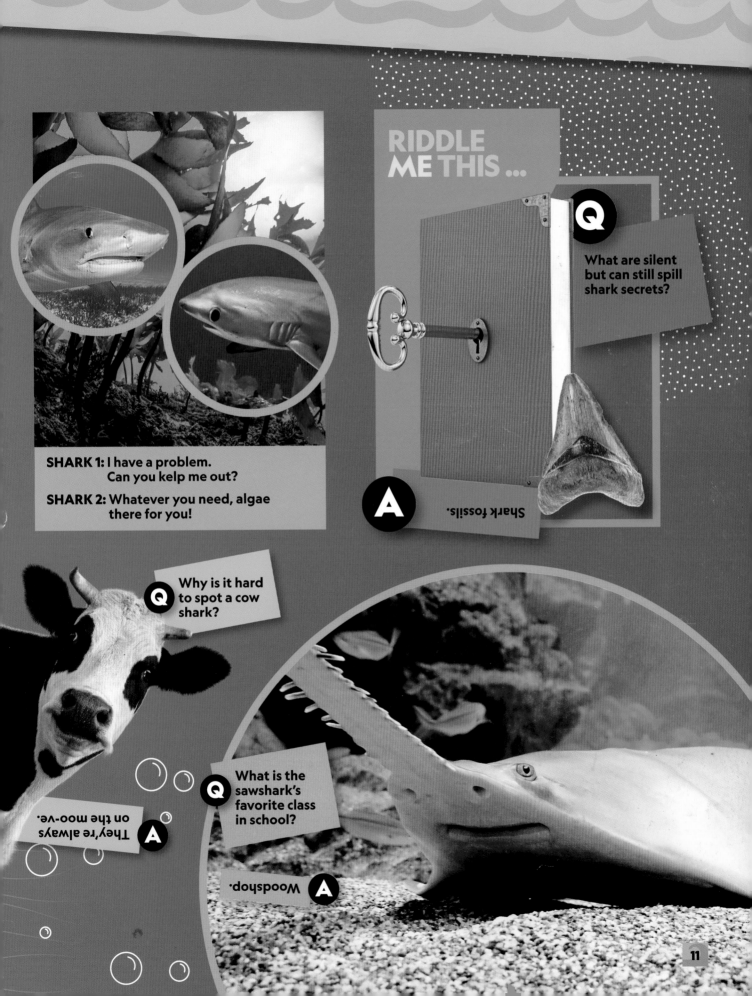

SHARK 1: I have a problem. Can you kelp me out?

SHARK 2: Whatever you need, algae there for you!

RIDDLE ME THIS ...

Q What are silent but can still spill shark secrets?

A Shark fossils.

Q Why is it hard to spot a cow shark?

A They're always on the moo-ve.

Q What is the sawshark's favorite class in school?

A Woodshop.

THE INS AND OUTS OF SHARKS

Sharks are cool inside and out! Their bodies are jam-packed with special parts that help them survive in the wild. Check out this drawing of a shark's body structure and get to the heart of what makes this fish tick.

Eyes
It is estimated that sharks can see about 10 times better than humans in dim light. Some sharks also have see-through eyelids. They can close the lids while swimming to protect their eyes from harm.

Snout
A shark's snout is covered in tiny pores. The pores can sense electrical currents given off by other animals. This helps sharks track down prey, even in the dark.

Skeleton
Sharks do not have bones. Instead, their skeletons are made of cartilage (CAR-tuh-lidge), a stretchy material found in living things, including in people's ears and noses. Light and flexible, the cartilage skeleton in sharks helps them move quickly through water.

Jaws
A shark's jaws are strong enough to crunch through bone. The jaws of some species are only loosely connected to the skull. These sharks can push their jaws forward to snag prey just out of reach!

Dorsal Fins
These top fins keep sharks upright as they swim. Most sharks have two dorsal fins, but some have only one.

Vertebrae
A shark's spine is made up of several linked pieces of cartilage called vertebrae. The vertebrae store energy. As the shark moves, some energy is released. This allows the shark to swim faster.

Lateral Line
This is a line of sensors along a shark's head and body. The sensors pick up on movement in the surrounding water. A shark uses the sensors to detect when predators are near.

Tail Fin
A shark uses its superstrong tail fin, also called a caudal (COD-al) fin, to push through the water.

Liver
A shark's liver is big and filled with oil. The oil is lighter than water. So, it helps to give the fish some buoyancy (BOY-un-see), or the ability to stay afloat.

Spiral Valve
This body part is in the intestines and is shaped like a corkscrew. The spiral valve helps sharks digest nutrients from food.

Gills
Like other fish, sharks use gills for breathing. As water passes over their gills, the gills take in a gas called oxygen. Oxygen is important for the survival of living organisms.

Pectoral Fins
These are a shark's side fins. Think of them a bit like the wings on an airplane. Sharks use these fins to stay balanced and to help steer through water.

THE SKINNY ON SHARK SKIN

SHARKS MAY BE TOP PREDATORS, BUT THEY still face

plenty of danger. Sharks can get scrapes from pointy rocks and coral. Or they can come across parasites, tiny organisms that can burrow into an animal's body and cause harm. Luckily, sharks have built-in armor to help keep them safe. What is this natural shield? Their skin! Get the scoop on this fish's spectacular surface.

SKIN FOR THE WIN!

Shark skin is covered in V-shaped scales called dermal denticles (DUR-muhl DEN-tih-cuhls). The scales tightly overlap one another. And they're made with a material similar to enamel, the same thing that coats your teeth! That means the scales are pretty strong. This tough skin is not easily scratched, and parasites have a hard time sticking to it.

A shark's skin doesn't just provide protection—it also gives the fish a boost of speed. Water flows smoothly over a shark's scales because of their shape. This allows the shark to move easily and quickly through water.

HELPING HUMANS

Scientists have been wowed by shark skin for years. And it's led people to develop cool products. Inventors have made swimsuits with material inspired by shark skin. They've also created a plastic material with tiny sharklike scales that can be used to cover things like door handles and elevator buttons. Real shark skin protects against germs, and this material is germ resistant, too. That means sharks are helping to keep *us* healthy. Thank you, sharks!

FIERCEST FEATURES

LOTS OF SHARKS HAVE COOL FEATURES, BUT THESE SHARKS HAVE SPECIAL BODY PARTS AND MOVES THAT MAKE THEM EXTRA FIERCE!

DEADLIEST HEAD MOVE

GREAT HAMMERHEAD SHARK

Named for its giant hammer-shaped head, the great hammerhead shark nails down its prey, often stingrays, to the bottom of the seafloor with mighty force. The prey wiggles around until it tires out. Then the hammerhead eats it.

SPEEDIEST TAIL WHIP

THRESHER SHARK

The thresher shark's tail looks like a long whip, making up half of its body length. It cracks its long tail as fast as 30 miles an hour (48 km/h)—though some have been known to whip as fast as 80 miles an hour (129 km/h). This whipping motion stuns several fish at once, with enough force to break them into pieces.

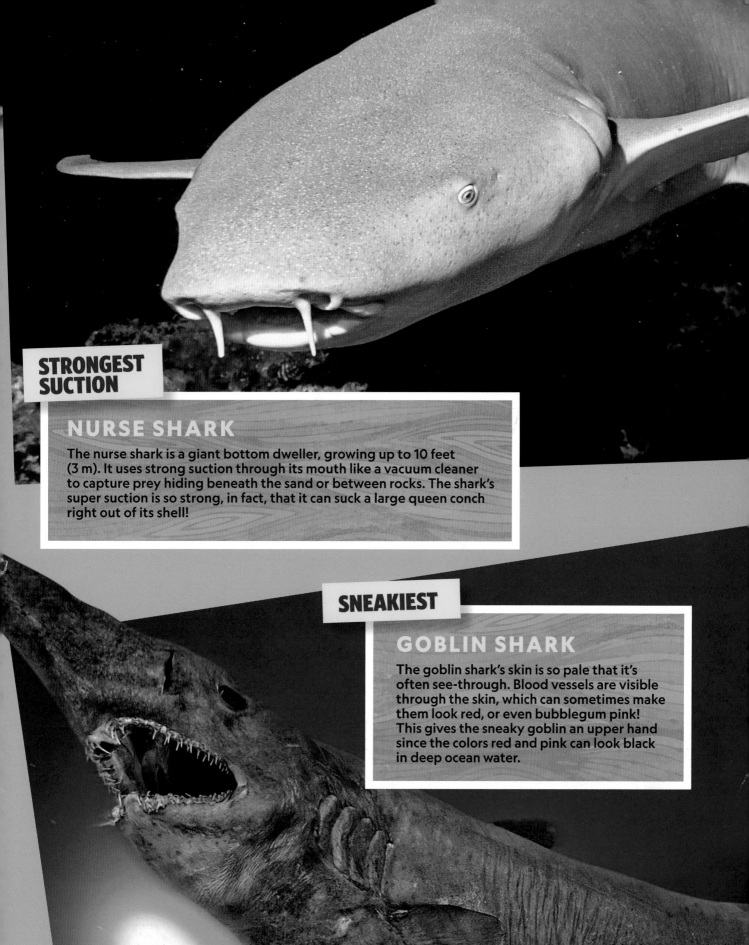

STRONGEST SUCTION

NURSE SHARK

The nurse shark is a giant bottom dweller, growing up to 10 feet (3 m). It uses strong suction through its mouth like a vacuum cleaner to capture prey hiding beneath the sand or between rocks. The shark's super suction is so strong, in fact, that it can suck a large queen conch right out of its shell!

SNEAKIEST

GOBLIN SHARK

The goblin shark's skin is so pale that it's often see-through. Blood vessels are visible through the skin, which can sometimes make them look red, or even bubblegum pink! This gives the sneaky goblin an upper hand since the colors red and pink can look black in deep ocean water.

HOME TURF

Earth's waters are filled with sharks! But different sharks have their own ranges. A range is the area where an animal species lives. Some kinds of sharks swim in the cold depths of the Arctic Ocean. Others soak up the sun in tropical waters. And still others span different areas across the planet. This map shows the places that five shark species call home.

Greenland Shark
Greenland sharks are usually found in the supercold waters of the North Atlantic and Arctic Oceans.

Great White Shark
These fish live throughout most oceans of the world. Although they are widespread, they tend to like waters with mild temperatures.

NORTH AMERICA

PACIFIC OCEAN

ATLANTIC OCEAN

SOUTH AMERICA

WHERE SHARKS LIVE
BASKING
GREAT WHITE
GREENLAND
SALMON
SAND TIGER

Sand Tiger Shark
Sand tiger sharks can be found in warm seas throughout the world. They usually live around continental shelves, which are shallow parts of the sea that run along big landmasses.

ARCTIC OCEAN

EUROPE

ASIA

AFRICA

PACIFIC OCEAN

INDIAN OCEAN

AUSTRALIA

0   2,000 mi
0   2,000 km

SOUTHERN OCEAN

ANTARCTICA

Salmon Shark
Found in the waters of the North Pacific, salmon sharks live between western North America and East Asia.

Basking Shark
The huge basking shark makes its home mostly in the Atlantic and Pacific Oceans.

MOST WELL-KNOWN SHARKS

The **TIGER SHARK'S** body is camouflaged by a striped and spotted pattern that makes the shark difficult to spot as it hunts for food.

The **BULL SHARK** starts its attack on prey like a bull on land—with a **POWERFUL HEADBUTT!**

The largest species of hammerhead shark is the great hammerhead, at 20 feet (6 m) long. The smallest is the bonnethead, at about four feet (1.2 m) long.

The **GREAT WHITE** is the world's largest predatory fish, meaning it hunts other animals to survive.

KNOWN TO HUNT IN GROUPS, BLUE SHARKS WILL WORK TOGETHER TO HERD WHOLE SCHOOLS OF FISH INTO A SMALL AREA AND TRAP THEM.

Sporting a
bullet-shaped snout,
the shortfin mako has the fastest bursts of speed of any shark in the sea.

The oceanic whitetip gets its name from ... you guessed it: its white-tipped fins.

Whale sharks swim with their giant mouths open so they can catch thousands of tiny, yummy plankton as they go.

WHICH SHARK WOULD BE YOUR BESTIE?

IF THESE DESCRIPTIONS DON'T FIT YOU, THAT'S OK. THIS QUIZ IS JUST FOR FUN!

Sharks have all sorts of different traits and preferences. So which shark do you have the most in common with? Answer these quiz questions and then add up your score to discover your shark soul mate.

1. What's your ideal vacation spot?

a. I'd love somewhere cold.

b. It must be warm.

c. I want wide open spaces.

d. It needs a great view.

e. I'd be happy almost anywhere.

2. What's your energy level?

a. I'm not fast, but I keep moving.

b. I save up my energy for when I need to kick it into high gear.

c. I like to lounge around.

d. I can be jumpy.

e. I feel the need for speed.

3. Are you super social or pretty private?

a. I love my privacy!

b. You'll find me with my crew most of the time.

c. I like to be in big crowds with new faces.

d. I like being with pals, but I try to stand out.

e. I'm not always private, but I like some "me time."

4. Friends would describe you as _____ .

a. brave

b. unique

c. kind

d. athletic

e. curious

5. Where can you be found at the pool?

a. mostly in the deep end

b. anywhere along the edge

c. the shallow end

d. in the air, after bouncing off the diving board

e. all over the place

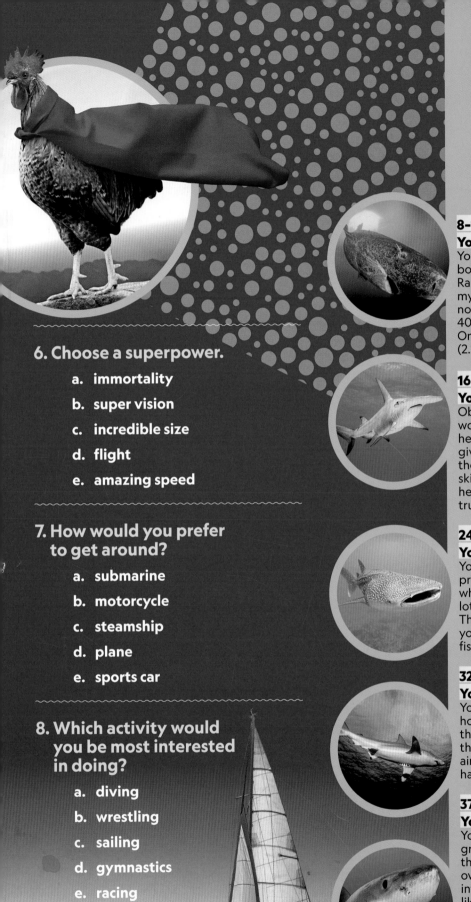

6. Choose a superpower.

a. immortality

b. super vision

c. incredible size

d. flight

e. amazing speed

7. How would you prefer to get around?

a. submarine

b. motorcycle

c. steamship

d. plane

e. sports car

8. Which activity would you be most interested in doing?

a. diving

b. wrestling

c. sailing

d. gymnastics

e. racing

ADD UP YOUR SCORE!
a = 1 b = 2 c = 3 d = 4 e = 5

8-15 Points
Your bestie is the Greenland shark.
You're on the private side but have a bold streak, just like the Greenland shark. Rarely seen, the fish is somewhat of a mystery. But we know it dwells in frigid northern waters and can live an estimated 400 years. It also dives to extreme depths. One was spotted more than 1.3 miles (2.2 km) underwater!

16-23 Points
Your bestie is the hammerhead shark.
Observant, clever, one of a kind. These words describe both you *and* a hammer-head! The position of the shark's eyes gives it 360-degree vision. That means they can see all around them. And these skilled, coastal-dwelling fish use their huge heads to pin down prey. These animals are truly unique, just like you.

24-31 Points
Your bestie is the whale shark.
You're kind and low-key but have a big presence. That's like the whale shark, which lives in warm, open waters or with lots of other marine life along coral reefs. This creature is calm and slow-moving, but you can't miss it. After all, it's the largest fish in the sea!

32-36 Points
Your bestie is the spinner shark.
You stand out from the crowd and know how to make a splash. Meet your match, the spinner shark. Traveling in groups, this fish often leaps from water into the air, rotating its body as it jumps. Spinners have really cool moves—just like you!

37-40 Points
Your bestie is the great white shark.
You're independent and curious. So are great whites! Found around the world, these creatures often travel on their own. And when they see something that interests them, they go check it out. Also like you, these speedy fish don't dawdle. In fact, they can swim up to 30 miles an hour (48 km/h)!

SHARK LOLs

KNOCK, KNOCK.

Who's there?
Reef.
Reef who?
I'm thirsty and would like a reef-freshment, please!

Q What do young sharks play at recess?

A Tide-and-seek.

Q What do you get when you cross a shark with a snowstorm?

A Frostbite.

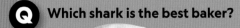

ALIYA: What would you say if you saw a zebra shark, a tiger shark, and a leopard shark swimming together?

HAKIM: I'd say, "It's a real zoo out there!"

LAUGHABLE LIST

Shark Picnic Menu

Peanut butter and jellyfish sandwiches

Krill-ed cheese

Sea cucumber salad

Crab-erry juice

TONGUE TWISTER

SAY THIS FAST THREE TIMES:
Bumbling bull sharks bump into boulders.

SHARK TIME TRAVELER

TSIORY ANDRIANAVALONA, PALEONTOLOGIST

Biologists find sharks in the ocean, but paleontologists like me study them from much higher in the mainland: no water around—just rocks and sand. That may seem a bit odd, but what I'm most passionate about is hunting for small shark teeth hidden and stuck in old rocks.

FINDING FOSSILS

When sharks die, they can be buried under sediment. Over millions of years, their teeth—and sometimes their vertebrae, or parts of their spine—are the only parts of sharks that are preserved. Those are my favorite treasures to find, and I am very good at treasure hunting! My teammates like to joke with me that since I'm not a tall person, my eyes are much closer to the ground. This can make it easier for me to find small fossils like shark teeth. What might seem like a flaw to others is actually a powerful reminder for me to always move forward.

THE DISCOVERY

One day, I was working at a difficult site. Under the hot sun, there was no clear path on the beach because the tide was getting higher and higher, so we jumped on rocks to go from one place to another. Suddenly, something shiny, sharp, and brown caught my eye. At first sight, I could tell this fossil was bigger than my usual finds. I got more and more excited as I dug it out of the rock using a hammer and a chisel. (I use those tools so often that my arms are super muscular after digging so much, day after day! So muscular in fact that I got the nickname "Rocket" from my teammates—I guess it is a reference to the wrestler "The Rock.")

Finally, I retrieved the fossil from the rock to find that it was evidence of a 23-million-year-old shark! By looking at its rare shape I could confirm that the tooth belonged to the species *Otodus megalodon*, a parent of the living great white shark.

ENDLESS TREASURES

Discoveries like this one make me super excited to be a paleontologist. In a certain way, finding and studying fossils is like having the superpower to go back in time, revealing the secret stories of sharks and an ancient environment that doesn't exist anymore.

MEGALODON TEETH ARE AS BIG AS AN ADULT HUMAN HAND AND CAN STILL BE FOUND ON BEACHES AROUND THE WORLD.

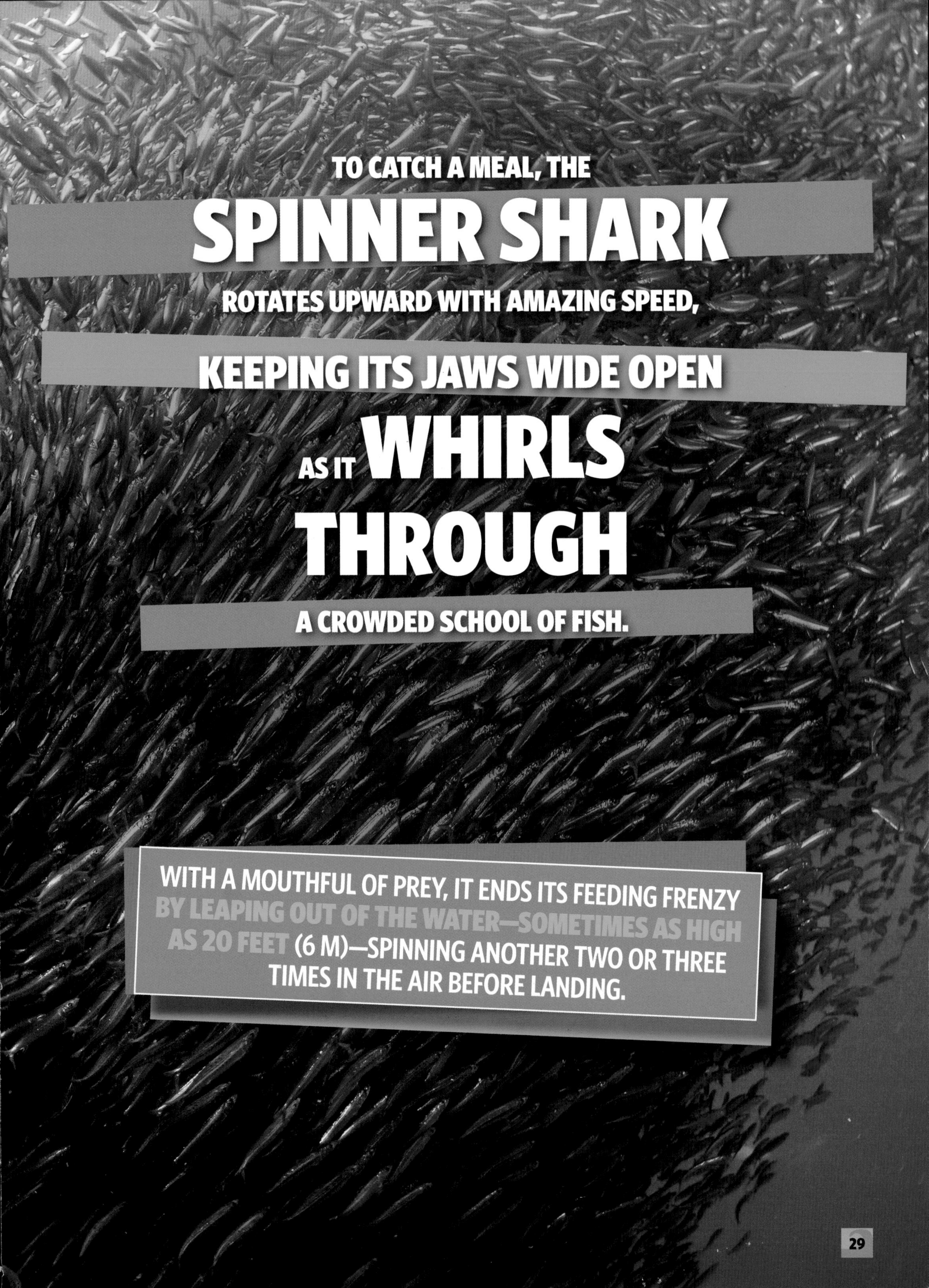

TO CATCH A MEAL, THE

SPINNER SHARK

ROTATES UPWARD WITH AMAZING SPEED,

KEEPING ITS JAWS WIDE OPEN

AS IT **WHIRLS**

THROUGH

A CROWDED SCHOOL OF FISH.

WITH A MOUTHFUL OF PREY, IT ENDS ITS FEEDING FRENZY BY LEAPING OUT OF THE WATER—SOMETIMES AS HIGH AS 20 FEET (6 M)—SPINNING ANOTHER TWO OR THREE TIMES IN THE AIR BEFORE LANDING.

SIZING UP SHARKS

Sharks come in all sizes, from giant to medium to itty-bitty. Want to find out just how big different species are? Take a look at the length of some sharks compared with some objects that match them in size. Then you can really see how these fish measure up to one another!

Whale Shark

LENGTH: More than 40 feet (12 m)

THAT'S ABOUT AS LONG AS: A large RV

Basking Shark

LENGTH: Around 30 feet (9 m)

THAT'S ABOUT AS LONG AS: 4 golf carts

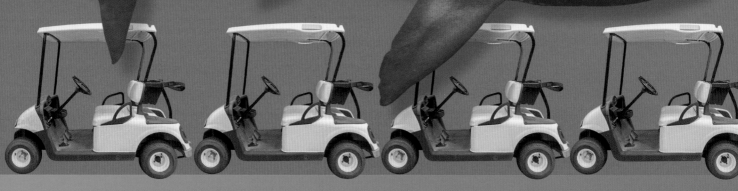

Great White Shark

LENGTH: Around 15 feet (4.5 m)

THAT'S ABOUT AS LONG AS: 3 baby grand pianos

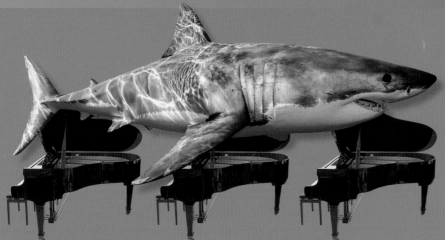

Nurse Shark
LENGTH: Around 7.5 feet (2 m)
THAT'S ABOUT AS LONG AS: 3 skateboards

Swell Shark
LENGTH: Around 3 feet (0.9 m)
THAT'S ABOUT AS LONG AS:
2 clothes hangers

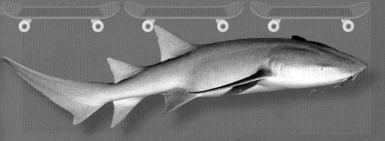

Blacktip Shark
LENGTH: Around 5 feet (1.5 m)
THAT'S ABOUT AS LONG AS: An adult-size hockey stick

Dwarf Lanternshark
LENGTH: Up to 7.9 inches (20 cm)
THAT'S ABOUT AS LONG AS: An unsharpened No. 2 pencil

THE LENGTHS GIVEN HERE ARE FOR FULL-GROWN ADULT SHARKS.

GREAT WHITE SHARKS

Great whites have special genes that help them **heal from severe wounds** in just a few weeks.

The shark's **torpedo-shaped body** allows it sudden bursts of speed reaching **30 miles** an hour (48 km/h) when it attacks prey.

THE "QUEEN OF THE OCEAN" IS A **3,541-POUND** (1,606-KG) GREAT WHITE SHARK THAT WAS DISCOVERED IN 2020 OFF THE COAST OF NOVA SCOTIA, CANADA.

Great whites are considered a **keystone species–** by eating so many fish, great whites keep the fish population from exploding!

USING TAGS to track great whites' movements is helping scientists discover parts of the ocean they didn't even know exist.

The "White Shark Café" is an area of the ocean roughly **the size of Colorado, U.S.A.,** where hundreds of great whites gather to dive deep for food.

GREAT WHITES CAN STAY WARM

WHEN ENTERING COLD WATER, making it easier for them to follow their favorite meal—seals—in and out of different temperature zones.

GREAT WHITE SHARKS CAN HAVE AS MANY AS

300 TEETH

IN THEIR JAWS AT ONCE.

Turn the page for more fearsome facts about great white sharks!

Great whites
CAN'T STOP SWIMMING
or they won't be able to breathe.

When they need to rest, great whites will **drift in the ocean with their mouths open** so that water can pass through their gills.

WITH A BITE FORCE OF UP TO 4,000 POUNDS PER SQUARE INCH (281 KG/SQ CM), A BITE FROM A GREAT WHITE WOULD FEEL LIKE BEING CRUSHED BY A CAR.

Great whites can live for about 30 years.

Great white sharks have rows of teeth at the ready. They can replace their front-row teeth with sharper and stronger ones as often as once a week.

The great white can sometimes be **found swimming as deep as 4,420 feet** (1,350 m)—that's nearly a mile below the surface!

The **LIGHT COLOR** of a great white's skin helps it hide in the water as it hunts.

The great white's scientific name, **Carcharodon** carcharias, means "ragged-toothed."

VOLCANO-DWELLING SHARKS

Not many brave the waters off the coast of the Solomon Islands, a nation in the South Pacific Ocean. Underneath them is one of the most active underwater volcanoes on Earth: Kavachi. If the volcano is more active than usual, eruptions will blow through the surface of the ocean and blast acid water and hot ash into the air. Scientists monitor the area to find out the safest times to sail toward the volcano, but the surrounding water is much too dangerous to get as close as they want. So how do they get around this? Underwater cameras and disposable robots!

KAVACHI VOLCANO IS OFTEN CALLED "SHARKCANO."

A SHOCKING SURPRISE

When a group of scientists dropped a camera into the crater of the volcano, they were in for a shocking surprise—there were dozens of scalloped hammerhead and silky sharks living in the volcano! Scientists weren't expecting to find much of any life down there, let alone sharks. First off, there's the danger of an eruption. Plus, the water around the volcano is very hot, acidic, and cloudy—not exactly the best elements for home sweet home.

MUTANT SHARKS

One theory suggests that the sharks must have mutated—changed from their original form—to adapt to this one-of-a-kind habitat. But the scientists still have more questions: Why is an active volcano worth living in when the risk is so high? What are the sharks drawn to? How much do sharks understand about their deadly surroundings? And what do they know and sense that we don't?

ROBOT EXPLOSION

When studying any harsh area, especially where volcanic eruptions take place, scientists have to be willing to part with their robots. This is because the robots aren't likely to survive an explosion. All they can hope for from their one-use robot is that it collects enough data before it's destroyed or that enough of it stays intact to keep any data it collects safe.

One thing is for sure: Scientists are gearing up all sorts of robotic tricks to make sure we learn more about these special sharks and their explosive habitat.

FISH FUNNIES

KANESHA: How does a shark clean its teeth?

ROHAN: I don't know. How?

KANESHA: Very carefully!

Q What does a shark say at the end of the day before falling asleep?

A "Good bite!"

Q Why do sea creatures love visiting a whale shark's home?

A Because it's so whale-coming.

TONGUE TWISTER

SAY THIS FAST THREE TIMES:

A goblin shark gobbles up gobs of goo.

SMALL FISH: How is your day?

SHARK: It's going swimmingly!

Q

What did the shark say when a downpour started?

A "It's raining catsharks and dogfish!"

Q Which shark performs in the orchestra?

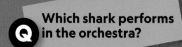

A The horn shark.

KNOCK, KNOCK.

Who's there?
Jaws.
Jaws who?
Have a jaws-some day!

MOTION MAGIC

All living creatures have electrical currents running through their bodies. Though humans can't sense other creatures' electrical currents, sharks do! That's because sharks have supersensitive pores called ampullae of Lorenzini. These mainly exist on the snout, but a unique portion running from their snouts to their tails is called the lateral line. The lateral line not only picks up electrical currents of prey, but also senses changes in water pressure, like the movement of a swimming fish or even the gentle vibrations of its heartbeat—sometimes from as far away as 330 feet (100 m). That's about as long as a football field! To better understand how a shark senses nearby prey, try this fun experiment.

YOU WILL NEED:

MILK
DISH SOAP
COTTON SWAB
FOOD DYE
SHALLOW BAKING DISH
GUMMY SHARK OR SMALL WATERPROOF OBJECT

STEP 1:

Fill the dish with half an inch (1.5 cm) of milk.

STEP 2:

Place the gummy shark or small waterproof object in the middle of the dish to act as the shark.

STEP 3:

Add a few dots of food coloring around the milk.

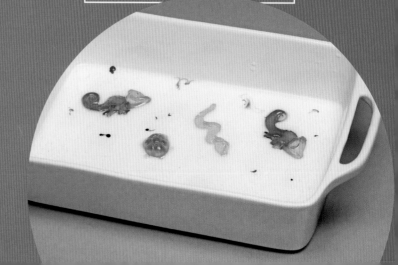

STEP 4:

Put a bit of dish soap on your cotton swab, then gently press the swab into one of the dots of color and watch the colors ripple away from the swab.

CONCLUSION:

Your cotton swab acts like an unsuspecting sea animal moving in nearby waters. The vibrations of the animal travel through the water—in this case, the colors growing outward from the swab. See how the colors suddenly meet up with the shark in the middle? Though the vibrations have no color in real life, a shark can feel them through its lateral line. From there, a shark fires up its other senses, like smell, to home in on the creature's (or swab's) location.

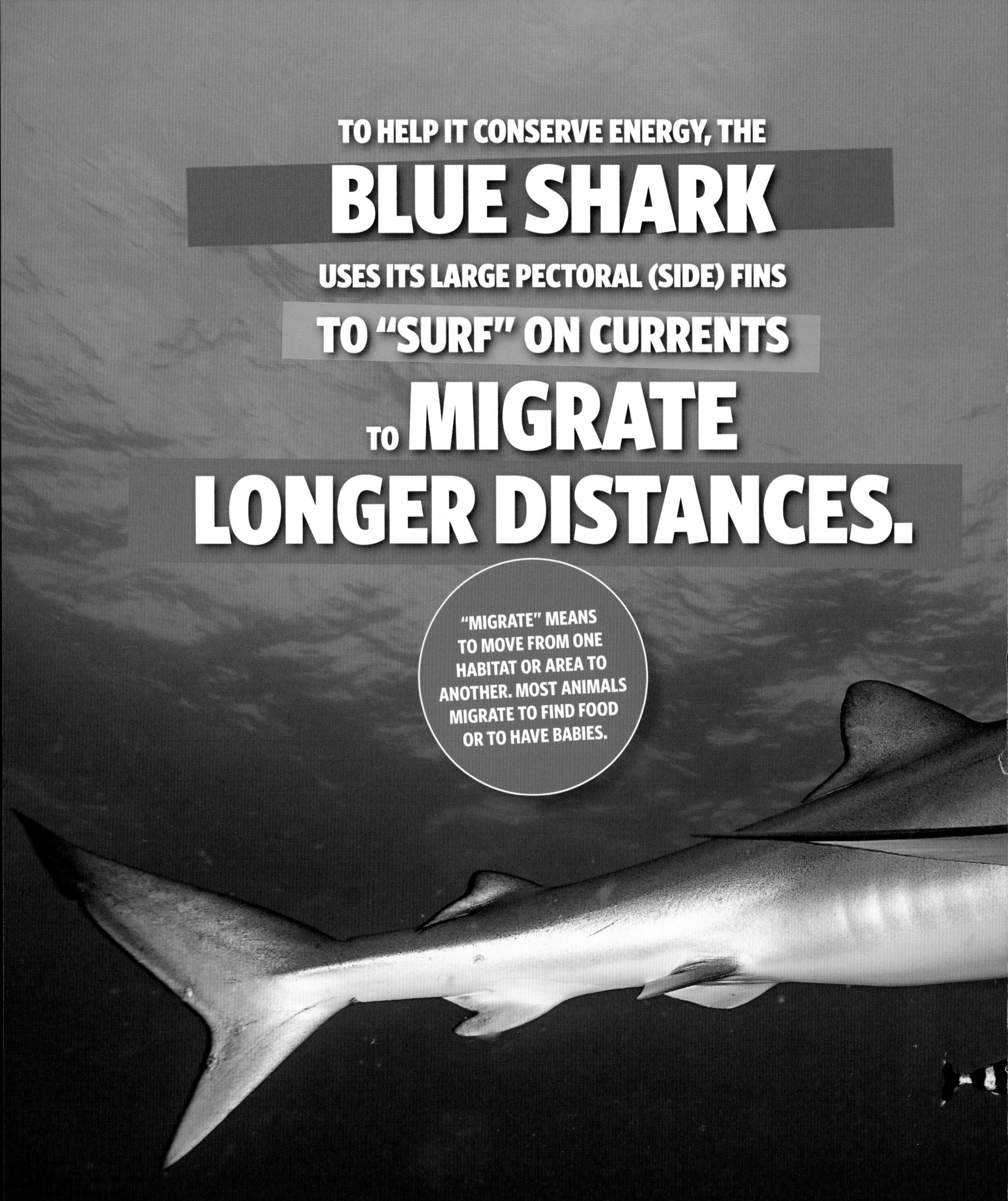

TO HELP IT CONSERVE ENERGY, THE

BLUE SHARK

USES ITS LARGE PECTORAL (SIDE) FINS

TO "SURF" ON CURRENTS

TO MIGRATE

LONGER DISTANCES.

"MIGRATE" MEANS
TO MOVE FROM ONE
HABITAT OR AREA TO
ANOTHER. MOST ANIMALS
MIGRATE TO FIND FOOD
OR TO HAVE BABIES.

BLUE SHARKS ARE FOUND ALL OVER THE WORLD EXCEPT AT THE NORTH AND SOUTH POLES.

SHARK SPA!

HOW DO OCEANIC WHITETIP SHARKS KEEP FRESH AND CLEAN?

They can't exactly get their fins on a bar of soap! Instead, they rely on pilot fish to clean them. Pilot fish and oceanic whitetips are often found swimming together in warm and tropical ocean waters. The animals are an unlikely match. A pilot fish is about 10 times smaller than an oceanic whitetip. As they travel, the pilot fish nibble up tiny living things called bacteria as well as bits of food on the shark's skin. The fish even swim inside the shark's mouth to clean its teeth. Yikes!

PILOT FISH PERKS

Pilot fish don't clean scraps from oceanic whitetips just to be nice. In return for their cleaning services, these fish get a yummy snack. In fact, many of their meals come from morsels of a shark's dinner that wound up on its skin. Swimming next to oceanic whitetips also provides the fish with some protection. After all, not many animals want to mess with a shark! Other sea creatures tend to steer clear of these sharks and the pilot fish that tag along with them.

SAFE AND SOUND

But do the sharks pose a danger to the pilot fish? Luckily, no. Oceanic whitetips know not to chomp down on their pilot fish cleaning crews. The sharks must *really* like getting their undersea spa treatments!

THESE SHARKS WEIGH UP TO 370 POUNDS (170 KG).

PILOT FISH WERE ONCE THOUGHT TO PILOT, OR LEAD, OTHER FISH TO FOOD. THAT'S HOW THEY EARNED THEIR NAMES.

SHARK LOLs

KNOCK, KNOCK.

Who's there?
Salmon.
Salmon who?
Can salmon give
me directions?
I'm lost.

Q What do you get when you cross a small-eye lanternshark with a blurred lanternshark?

A A shark that really needs some glasses!

SHARK 1: Was the reef crowded today?

SHARK 2: We were packed in like sardines!

Q What kind of stories do threshers tell?

A Tall tails.

TONGUE TWISTER

SAY THIS FAST THREE TIMES: A snoozing shark snores soundly in the sea.

YOU'VE GOT TO BE JOKING ...

Q Where do sharks do their studying?

A In schools of fish.

PALEONTOLOGIST 1: Look at this huge shark fossil.

PALEONTOLOGIST 2: That fish makes quite an impression!

SURPRISING SIGHT

THESE SHARKS HAVE THE MOST EYE-CREDIBLE STORIES TO TELL!

COOLEST EYE PATCH

TIGER SHARK

Avast ye, shark lovers! More rad than any pirate's eye patch, many sharks, such as the tiger shark, have what is considered a third eyelid. It is a clear layer called the nictitating membrane that "closes," allowing a shark to see while protecting its eyes from any damage that could happen when it's attacking panicked prey.

WIDEST VIEW

GREAT HAMMERHEAD SHARK

The wider the great hammerhead's head, the greater its binocular vision will be—this is when two eyes focus on an object to create a single image. Sound familiar? That's because humans have binocular vision, too! But because hammerhead eyes are set so wide apart, their fields of vision overlap, giving them a 360-degree view of their underwater world.

SPOOKIEST EYE TRICK

GREAT WHITE SHARK

The great white has gifted sight. It can see during the day and at night—anything for a fresh bite! But when its prey tries to put up a fight, the great white doesn't have a third eyelid to protect its eyes like its buddy the tiger shark. Instead, the great white rolls its pupils to the back of its head, showing only the ghostly whites of its eyes. *Eeek!* It finishes the kill using its other strong senses, like smell.

SANDBAR SHARK

The sandbar shark sports skinny vertical slits for pupils that likely adapt quickly to light and dark areas, especially when hunting— but the mysteries of how, when, and why are still to be discovered. It can be difficult to study sharks that are more active at night, so for now some scientists compare the sandbar shark's pupils to those of a cat. Cats have vertical slits that can grow to a whopping three times the size of a human's pupil at night. This helps them see clearer and farther—ready for action!

MOST MYSTERIOUS EYES

WHAT IN THE WORLD?

These photos show close-up views of animals that live in shark territory. Unscramble the letters to identify what's in each picture. Answers are at the bottom of page 51.

1

XOOLATL

2

RAOCL

3

BCRA

4

ESA ROTET

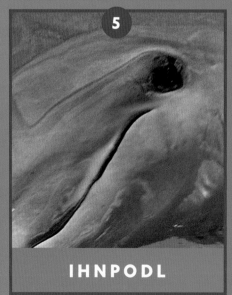

5

IHNPODL

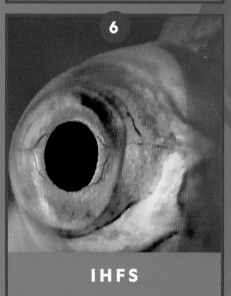

6

IHFS

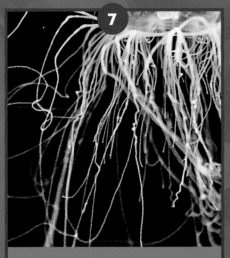

7

SFELHLIJY

8

FHUFSERFIP

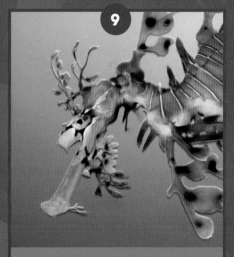

9

ASE NOGADR

10

LSRWUA

11

SAE ELTTRU

12

ESA RTAS

13

HRMIPS

14

RCAO

15

SHETFTLICU

SUPER-STRANGE SHARKS

Compared to its body length, the **winghead** has the widest head of all hammerhead species— nearly as wide as half its body length!

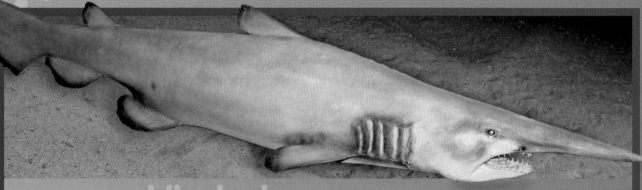

The **goblin shark** is named after a demonlike creature from Japanese folklore that has a very long nose.

THE **angel shark** USES ITS WINGLIKE FINS TO BURY ITSELF IN THE SAND AND SURPRISE ATTACK PREY THAT SWIMS ABOVE IT.

Basking sharks have the largest pups at six feet (1.8 m) long—that's the length of two Great Danes!

The small **viper dogfish** shark has jaws that spring outward to catch its prey.

TO ATTRACT UNSUSPECTING PREY, A **MEGAMOUTH** SHARK'S MOUTH HAS A WHITE BAND ACROSS IT THAT REFLECTS THE LIGHT OF ITS GLOWING PREY TO TRICK IT.

At only 1.5 feet (0.5 m) long, the tiny cookiecutter shark's bite has been powerful enough to damage nuclear submarines, forcing humans to create shark-resistant coverings.

With a life span that's estimated at **400 years,** the Greenland shark is one of the **longest-living creatures** on the planet.

The **sawshark slashes** its swordlike sharp-toothed snout from side to side to stun its prey.

The **frilled shark** was named for the fancy ruffled gills around its neck.

THE FOUR-FOOT (1.2-M)

TASSELED WOBBEGONG

HAS TASSELS THAT RESEMBLE A

RUG AND MIMIC CORAL-LIKE BRANCHES

TO **TRICK**

PREY.

THIS FLAT SHARK'S FANCY PATTERN OF WHITE SPOTS BREAKS UP THE SHAPE OF ITS BROWNISH BODY AGAINST THE OCEAN FLOOR, WHICH MAKES IT HARD TO SPOT.

QUIZ TIME

IF YOU'RE STUMPED BY A QUESTION, YOU CAN LOOK THROUGH THE FIRST HALF OF THE BOOK TO FIND THE ANSWER!

1 What is a whale shark's favorite snack?

a. plankton

b. waffles

c. large fish

d. seaweed

2 What shape are a sandbar shark's pupils?

a. large circles

b. skinny slits

c. small triangles

d. thin squiggles

3 Scientists estimate that Greenland sharks can live _____ .

a. around 50 years

b. around 120 years

c. around 400 years

d. forever

4 Which oily body part helps a shark to float?

a. its heart

b. its bladder

c. its stomach

d. its liver

5 Which shark pins down prey with its head?

a. the lemon shark

b. the nurse shark

c. the hammerhead shark

d. the Pacific sleeper shark

6 What do the pores in a shark's snout detect?

a. ripples of moving ships

b. electrical currents from prey

c. scents of other animals

d. sounds made by nearby sharks

7 Where are sharks' dorsal fins?

a. on their sides

b. on their backs

c. on their bellies

d. in their noses

8 Which shark has see-through skin?

a. the goblin shark

b. the window shark

c. the whale shark

d. the sand tiger shark

9 What do pilot fish do to help oceanic whitetips?

a. lead them to prey

b. scratch their itches

c. clean food off them

d. shield them from bigger fish

10 How fast can a thresher shark whip its tail?

a. up to 20 miles an hour (32 km/h)

b. up to 40 miles an hour (64 km/h)

c. up to 80 miles an hour (129 km/h)

d. up to 100 miles an hour (161 km/h)

11 Which sharks have been known to bite the outside of submarines?

a. dwarf lanternsharks

b. great white sharks

c. bull sharks

d. cookiecutter sharks

SNEAKIEST DEFENSES

SHARKS HAVE AMAZING WAYS OF PROTECTING THEMSELVES.

COOLEST LIGHT TRICK

DWARF LANTERNSHARK

Since the dwarf lanternshark is small enough to rest in a human hand, it needs to be at the ready to fight off predators at all times! That's why the glow of its itty-bitty belly and fins comes to save the day. When feeding in shallow water, the light it emits helps it blend into the sunlight. On the other hand, in deep dark water, that same glow is used to lure in prey. Tricky little fellow!

BEST BUILT-IN FORT

PUFFADDER SHYSHARK

Named after the puffadder snake because of its similar skin pattern, this shark can easily blend in with the seafloor, where it preys on crustaceans. But, being a small shark, the puffadder is often prey—hunted by seals, birds, and other sharks. To protect itself from predators, the puffadder shyshark will curl into a circle like a sleepy puppy and cover itself with its tail, making it harder for predators to swallow.

SWELL SHARK

Like the puffadder shark, the swell shark blends in well with its surroundings. When the swell shark feels threatened, it curls into a U-shape and bites on to its own tail. Then it swallows a bunch of sea-water, which makes it double its size! This makes it difficult for predators to bite the swell shark, and if it happens to be between two rocks, the swelling makes it nearly impossible for the shark to be removed.

MOST TOXIC BITE

HORN SHARK

Horn sharks are famous for swimming slowly, which means they're often easy prey for other predators—or so those predators think. Horn sharks are one of only two venomous sharks on the planet! Both the horn shark and the spiny dogfish sport long swordlike spikes on their two dorsal fins, but horn sharks take the venom cake with one more spike on the anal fin. These spikes provide a toxic blow to predators while also making them hard to swallow—ouch!

PREHISTORIC SHARKS

THE **MEGALODON** IS THE BIGGEST SHARK EVER KNOWN TO HAVE LIVED. IT IS ESTIMATED TO HAVE BEEN UP TO 60 FEET (18.3 M) LONG.

Squalicorax likely fed on dead land animals that wound up in the ocean— even the giant *T. rex!*

Edestus

is known as the scissor-tooth shark because it used its **serrated jaws**—puckered outward like a duck's bill—to slash and thrash its prey.

Ptychodus, aka the **crusher shark,** had a whopping 550 flat teeth to crush large amounts of shellfish at once.

Stethacanthus is known as the

ANVIL SHARK

because instead of being shaped like a triangle, its dorsal fin was shaped like a spike-covered anvil.

Cretoxyrhina mantelli, nicknamed the

GINSU SHARK

after a brand of swift chopping knives, was a fierce shark whose fossils have been found in Kansas, U.S.A.— a landlocked state!

Cladoselache

is known as the first true shark, but it had no scales or denticles like

modern-day sharks.

SALTY GUMMY BEARS

Most sharks are made to exist in salty ocean water, which is why it is rare to see a shark in a freshwater environment, like a river. If an average shark were to wander into a river, its body would get confused and wouldn't be able to hold the right amount of salt, which could make its cells bloat and rupture.

To understand how important salt is to a shark, try this fun and easy gummy bear experiment!

STEP 1:
Pour one cup of water in each container.

YOU WILL NEED:
GUMMY BEARS
2 CUPS (475 ML) WATER
2 TABLESPOONS (35 G) SALT
2 CONTAINERS (PREFERABLY CLEAR SO YOU CAN SEE THE GUMMY BEARS IN ACTION)

STEP 2:
Add two tablespoons of salt to only one container and give it a quick stir. Leave the other container with water only.

SALT WATER

PLAIN WATER

CONCLUSION:
At the end of the experiment, you'll see that the gummy bear in the plain water has become extremely bloated, much like what would happen to an average shark if it left the ocean and entered freshwater (a river). On the other hand, the gummy bear resting in salt water (the ocean) has been able to keep its form better, staying much more dense.

STEP 3:
Place one gummy bear in each container.

STEP 4:
Wait overnight to see results. Wait a second night for even more obvious results.

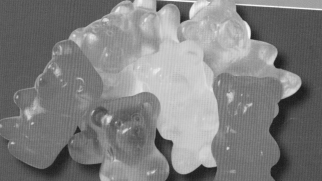

FISH FUNNIES

KNOCK, KNOCK.

Who's there?
Water.
Water who?
Water your favorite sharks? Mine are great whites!

Q Why do Greenland sharks like living in cold waters?

A Because they're so chill.

Q Why don't sharks like fast food?

A Because they can't catch it!

TONGUE TWISTER

SAY THIS FAST THREE TIMES:

A tiger shark does twirls with a troop of turtles.

BEN: What do you get when you cross a milk shark with a spinner shark?

MARIANNA: I don't know. What?

BEN: A milkshake shark!

YOU'VE GOT TO BE JOKING ...

Q Where do ghost sharks hang out?

A At their favorite haunts.

Q What do you call a greedy shark?

A A selfish.

Q What do you call a wobbegong that loves to exercise?

A A wobbe-strong.

BASKING SHARK MYSTERY

LUCY A. HAWKES, PHYSIOLOGICAL ECOLOGIST

Even though basking sharks are huge (they can get up to 30 feet [9 m] long) and they come to the waters of the United Kingdom every year, nobody knows where they go to have babies. This is a problem because basking sharks are in danger of being erased from our planet. To help their species recover, we want to protect the places they find the most important, like the places where they breed.

SHARK SPOTTING

To find out, we've been attaching specially designed cameras to the sharks, using a giant window-cleaning pole while leaning over the front of a big boat. It's very exciting! So far, our cameras have filmed the sharks gathering together in the early hours of the morning, touching pectoral fins like they are checking each other out. We've also filmed them jumping clear out of the water, possibly to show off to each other!

A THRILLING ADVENTURE

One of the most exciting bits of my job is hanging over the edge of a boat trying to attach the tracking tags! Since the sharks are too big to catch, we have to sneak up behind them to attach the tag. It's hard—the pole is heavy, the tag is really expensive, and you only have seconds to choose where to attach the tag and go for it! But when we get the data back from the tag we can see where the sharks have been, what they have been doing, and where the most important parts of the ocean are for them—which means we can protect them. It is so thrilling to get so close to such a HUGE animal that not that many people get to see.

Applying the tracking tag

Close-up of the tracking tag

A PHYSIOLOGICAL ECOLOGIST STUDIES THE WAY ANIMALS ADAPT TO CHANGING ENVIRONMENTS.

SHARKS ARE JUST LIKE US

HUMANS AND SHARKS MIGHT HAVE MORE IN COMMON THAN YOU THINK!

Research shows that lemon sharks share some of the same traits as people. They make friends. They learn by watching others. And they have individual personalities. That's a lot like us!

SHARK BFFs

Scientists at the Bimini Shark Lab in the Bahamas have observed lemon sharks for years. For one study, they placed colored tags on lemon sharks in the area to tell them apart. After watching them closely, the scientists noticed that the same sharks always swam and spent time together. They realized that the fish in each group must be friends!

BABY LEMON SHARKS LIVE IN GROUPS CALLED NURSERIES.

LEMON SHARKS USUALLY BEFRIEND OTHER LEMON SHARKS OF THE SAME SIZE.

WATCH AND LEARN!

Lemon sharks don't just swim with their friends. They also learn from them. In one experiment, scientists trained some lemon sharks to gently bump into a target. When they did so, the fish got a snack. Then other sharks were placed with the trained ones. The untrained sharks watched their trained pals hit the target for food—and some were able to copy this behavior!

FROM BOLD TO SHY

Studying groups of shark buddies has revealed something else. Scientists noticed that in each group, some sharks are bold. They often take the lead, swimming at the front of the pack. Other sharks are cautious. They usually hang in the back. This tells the scientists that the sharks have different personalities, just as humans do.

WHICH SHARK HANGOUT IS RIGHT FOR YOU?

Sharks dwell at different ocean depths, from very shallow to super-duper deep. (Check out the sidebar for more details.) Which depth would you like most? Answer these quiz questions. Then add up your score to discover where in the sea you'd be if you suddenly turned into a shark!

1. What's your favorite time of day?

a. daytime

b. dusk

c. nighttime

2. How much do you like the spotlight?

a. Attention, everyone: I love being noticed!

b. Sometimes I like it, other times I don't.

c. Keep the spotlight far away from me, please.

3. What's your adventure level?

a. I like being surrounded by the familiar.

b. A balance of adventure and calmness is key.

c. I'm always ready to explore the unknown!

4. Which animals are you most fascinated by?

a. dolphins

b. jellyfish

c. sea spiders

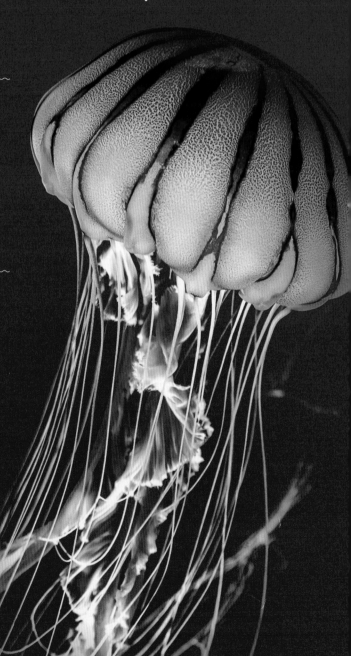

The Dirt on Ocean Depths

The ocean is divided into different zones, which are layered like a cake. On top, you've got the sunlit zone. Next comes the twilight zone. Finally, there's the midnight zone, the deepest part. All the zones have cool features, and each comes with some pretty awesome sharks!

The Sunlit Zone

The Twilight Zone

The Midnight Zone

5. How do you feel about crowds?

    a. **The bigger the crowd, the better.**

    b. **Every once in a while, they're good.**

    c. **I like my space.**

ADD UP YOUR SCORE!
a = 1 b = 2 c = 3

7-11 Points
The Sunlit Zone
Your ocean home is the warmest and most light-filled part of the sea. You share your not-so-deep digs with plenty of animals, including lots of sharks. Here, lemon sharks swim in knee-deep waters in bays and reefs. And blue sharks and threshers zip through in the open ocean.

6. What's your ideal weather?

    a. **I like things on the warm side.**

    b. **Keep it cold!**

    c. **Believe it or not, freezing days are my thing.**

Lemon shark

12-17 Points
The Twilight Zone
Welcome to your perfect undersea hangout! It's cold, dim, and home to a few odd critters. Here, the chain catshark uses its glow-in-the-dark skin as a built-in nightlight. Your other twilight zone neighbors include the bluntnose sixgill shark and the gulper shark, a fish with huge green eyes.

7. How fast can you swim?

    a. **Not to brag, but I'm very fast!**

    b. **My speed is set to medium.**

    c. **Slow and steady wins the race.**

Catshark

Goblin shark

18-21 Points
The Midnight Zone
The midnight zone is on the extreme side. Your ocean hangout is super deep, dark, and cold. In this zone, you may bump into goblin sharks that creep through the pitch-black depths. These are some of the deep-sea animals we know about. Many others have yet to be discovered.

SHARK LOLs

Q Where do sharks go to see movies?

A The dive-in.

Q What does a shortfin mako shark always want to eat?

A Mako-roni and cheese.

Q Who takes care of fish when they have a cold?

A A nurse shark.

LAUGHABLE LIST

Sharks' Favorite Stories

Snow White and the Seven Dwarf Lanternsharks

Rumpel-shark-skin

The Three Little Pygmy Sharks

Beauty and the Basking Shark

The Swordfish in the Stone

SHARK 1: Will you come for a swim with me?

SHARK 2: Shore thing!

KNOCK, KNOCK.

Who's there?
Fish.
Fish who?
It's o-fish-al ... I love sharks!

TOOTH TRACKER

Here's something to chew on: Many sharks sport five to 15 rows of teeth—and some have even more. That's a lot of chompers! These teeth vary in size and shape depending on the shark species they belong to. Brush up on your knowledge of shark teeth with these pictures of pearly whites from various species.*

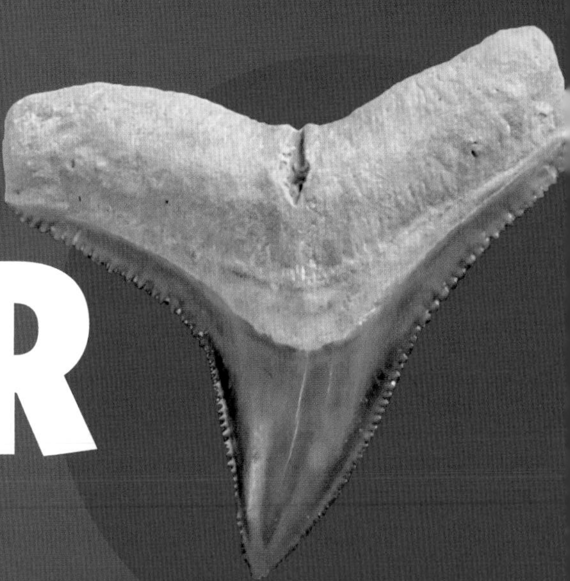

BULL SHARK

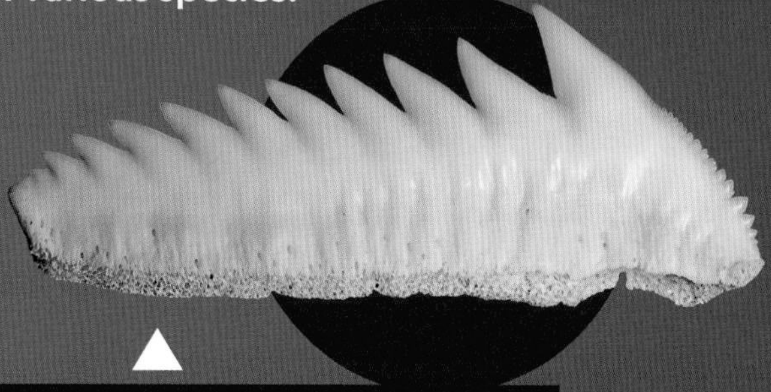

BLUNTNOSE SIXGILL SHARK

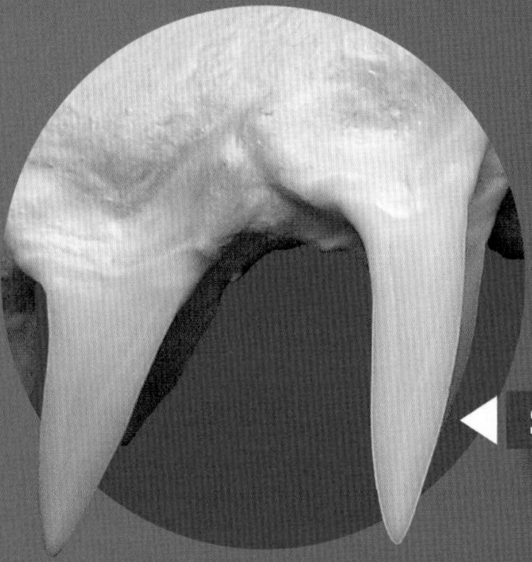

SHORTFIN MAKO SHARK

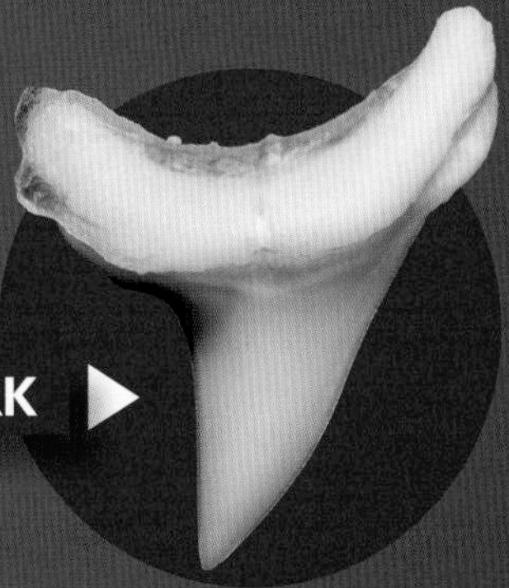

COMMON THRESHER SHARK

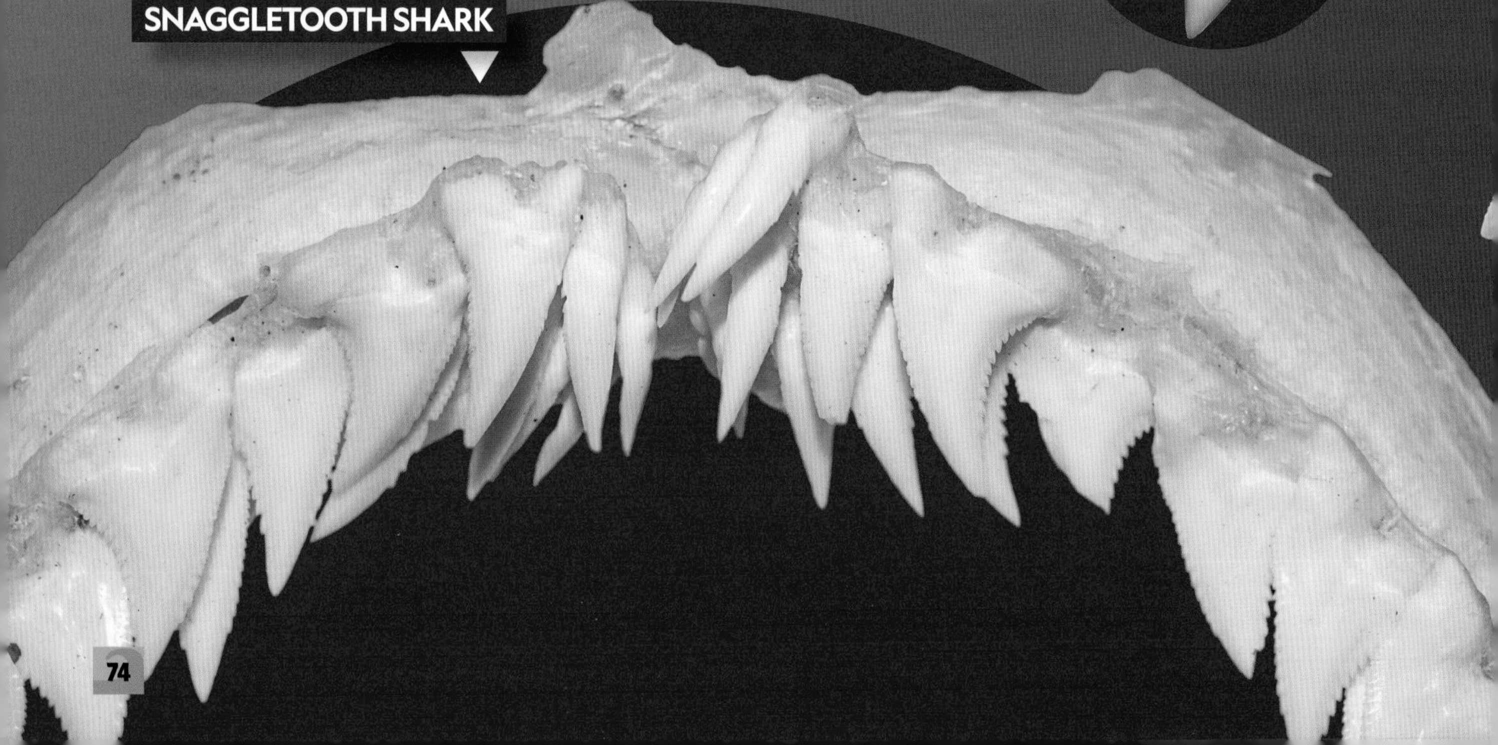

SNAGGLETOOTH SHARK

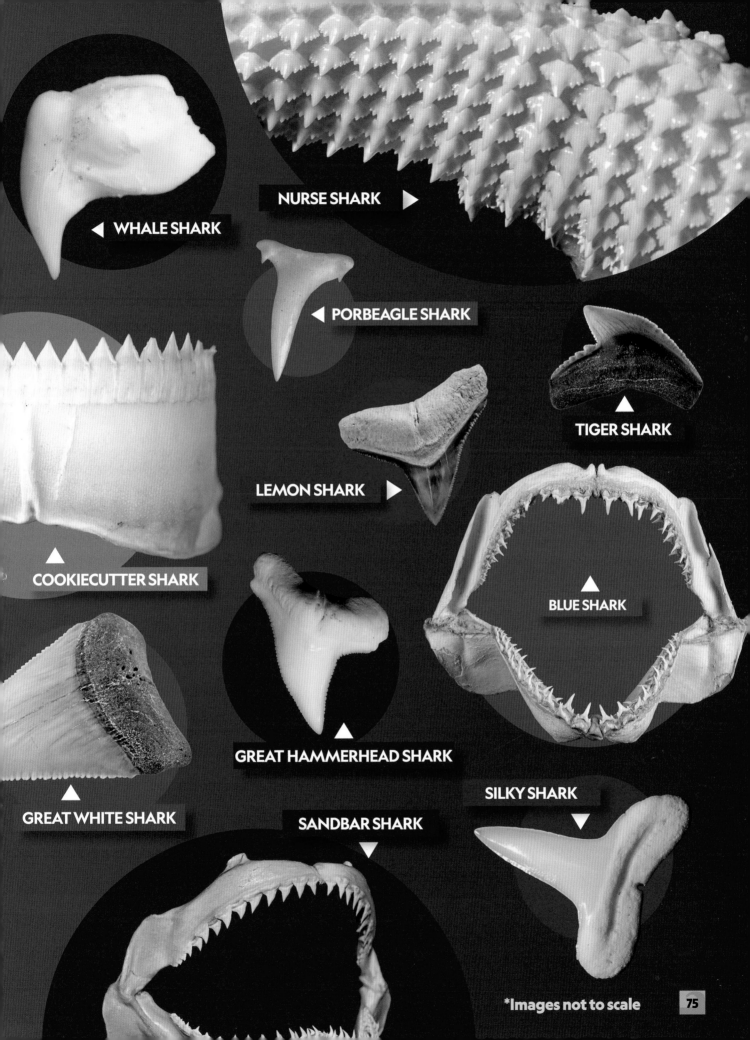

WHALE SHARK

NURSE SHARK ▶

◀ PORBEAGLE SHARK

TIGER SHARK ▲

COOKIECUTTER SHARK ▲

LEMON SHARK ▶

BLUE SHARK ▲

GREAT HAMMERHEAD SHARK ▲

SILKY SHARK ▽

GREAT WHITE SHARK ▲

SANDBAR SHARK ▽

*Images not to scale

JAW-SOME TEETH

Bull sharks have around **50 rows** of teeth.

WHEN SHARKS LOSE A TOOTH IN THE FRONT ROW, A TOOTH FROM THE BACK ROW **PUSHES FORWARD** IN ITS PLACE, AND A NEW TOOTH STARTS TO GROW IN THE BACK.

The **cookiecutter shark** pierces its prey with its sharp triangular bottom teeth then rotates its entire body to cut out a perfect piece of cookie-shaped flesh.

The hooked bottom teeth of the snaggletooth shark jut out from its mouth. It can easily spear prey to hold it in place while the top teeth shred the prey to pieces.

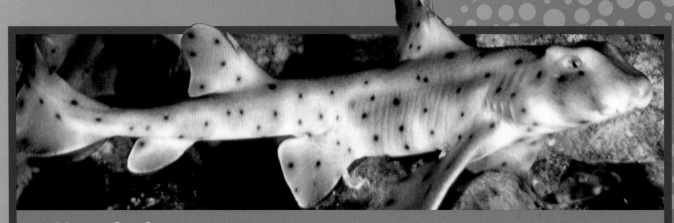

Horn sharks eat so many sea urchins, their teeth are often stained purple.

TIGER SHARK TEETH ARE STRONG ENOUGH TO CRACK THE SHELLS OF SEA TURTLES.

Wobbegong sharks will sometimes hold prey in their teeth for a few days before it dies.

Some sharks can go through as many as **20,000 teeth** in a lifetime.

Nurse sharks suck in their prey like **a vacuum,** using their several rows of teeth to clamp down on the prey, then swallow it whole.

Hammerhead shark

MANY SHARKS, LIKE THE SCALLOPED HAMMERHEAD AND THE FRILLED SHARK, HAVE ROWS OF BACKWARD-FACING TEETH TO KEEP PREY FROM ESCAPING ONCE IT'S IN THEIR MOUTH!

SHARK SCRAMBLE

These shark names look a little fishy. That's because the letters have been jumbled! Unscramble the letters in each name to identify the type of shark pictured. Write your answers on a separate piece of paper. Then compare them to the answer key at the bottom of the page. Ready, set, play!

1

2

EDAMEAHHRM

SHARKS WERE ONCE KNOWN AS SEA DOGS.

3

UBLE AKSRH

Answers: 1. sawshark, 2. hammerhead, 3. blue shark, 4. spotted wobbegong, 5. whale shark, 6. shortfin mako, 7. oceanic whitetip, 8. sand tiger shark

ETSTOPD GENBBOOGW

HAKWSARS

4

MORE THAN 500 SHARK SPECIES LIVE ON EARTH.

5

WELHA SRHAK

ONSRITHF MAOK

6

7

ECANOCI TWPHIIET

8

ASDN RGETI SAHKR

PICTURE THIS

CLICK, CLICK, CLICK.

A photographer in a diving suit snaps pics of a basking shark weaving through water. This fish has no idea it's part of a photo shoot. Suddenly, the shark circles around to face the human. They stare at each other for a heart-stopping moment. Then the shark slips away. Taking photos of sharks is exciting work. But it's not easy. Find out how the photographers do it!

SPLASHY SHOTS

Shark photographers must be skilled divers. And they need the right tools. They sport scuba suits, masks, and other diving gear as they work. They also often wear belts with weights to keep from floating to the surface. And, of course, they have a waterproof camera! The water may be murky. So, when a shark zips by, the photographer must swim close for a clear shot. Photographers can stay underwater only for short chunks of time. That means they must act fast.

TRICKY PICS

Taking photos of wild animals can be risky. So photographers sometimes snap shark photos from inside a cage. Other times, they get the sharks to come to them! To do this, they may use an object that's shaped like a seal. They attach it to their boat with a cord and drag it through the water. Thinking the object might be a snack, curious sharks swim over to check it out. Then the photographers take close-ups of the animals from the boat.

PHOTOGRAPHER BRIAN SKERRY HAS SPENT MORE THAN 10,000 HOURS UNDERWATER SNAPPING PICTURES OF SHARKS AND OTHER SEA CREATURES!

SOME PHOTOGRAPHERS USE MOVIE LIGHTS TO BRIGHTEN THE WATER WHILE TAKING SHARK PHOTOS.

REMORA FISH USE AN ORGAN ON THEIR HEADS THAT WORKS LIKE A SUCTION CUP TO HITCH A RIDE ON A WHALE SHARK'S BODY!

WHALE SHARKS

HAVE HUNDREDS OF TINY TOOTHLIKE SCALES

ON THEIR EYEBALLS

THAT PROTECT THEM

FROM HARMFUL OBJECTS AND

ATTACKS.

MEOW-GICAL CATSHARK GLOW

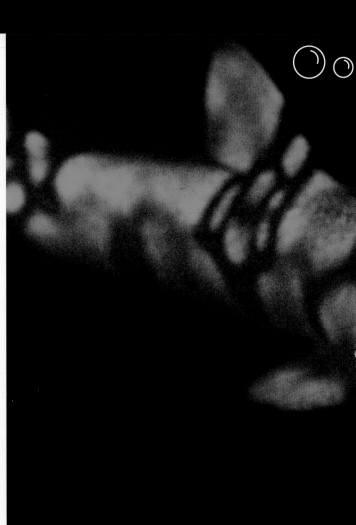

NEARLY THREE-QUARTERS OF ALL SEA ANIMALS CREATE THEIR OWN LIGHT.

They use these special glowing powers to communicate, attract mates, and even trick predators, especially in deep waters where barely any sunlight can reach and animals cautiously swim in the cold dark waters.

LIGHT IT UP!

Bioluminescence (by-oh-loom-in-ESS-ence) is when animals create this light through a chemical reaction within their body. Biofluorescence (by-oh-floor-ESS-ence) is when an animal's skin has the power to absorb blue light (the color of sunlight when it enters the sea) and send the light back out as a different color.

Catsharks emit, or give off, light through biofluorescence, but with a twist! Scientists discovered surprising new molecules that change the way catsharks glow. Instead of glowing in one big blob, catsharks use these molecules to glow in specific patterns. Females and males have different patterns.

FISH ARMOR

But that's not all! The newly discovered molecules likely protect catsharks from disease and toxic algae—a clever suit of fish armor that battles infection. Amazingly, even fish can get sunburned from light that enters the water, and the catshark molecules likely keep them from getting burned.

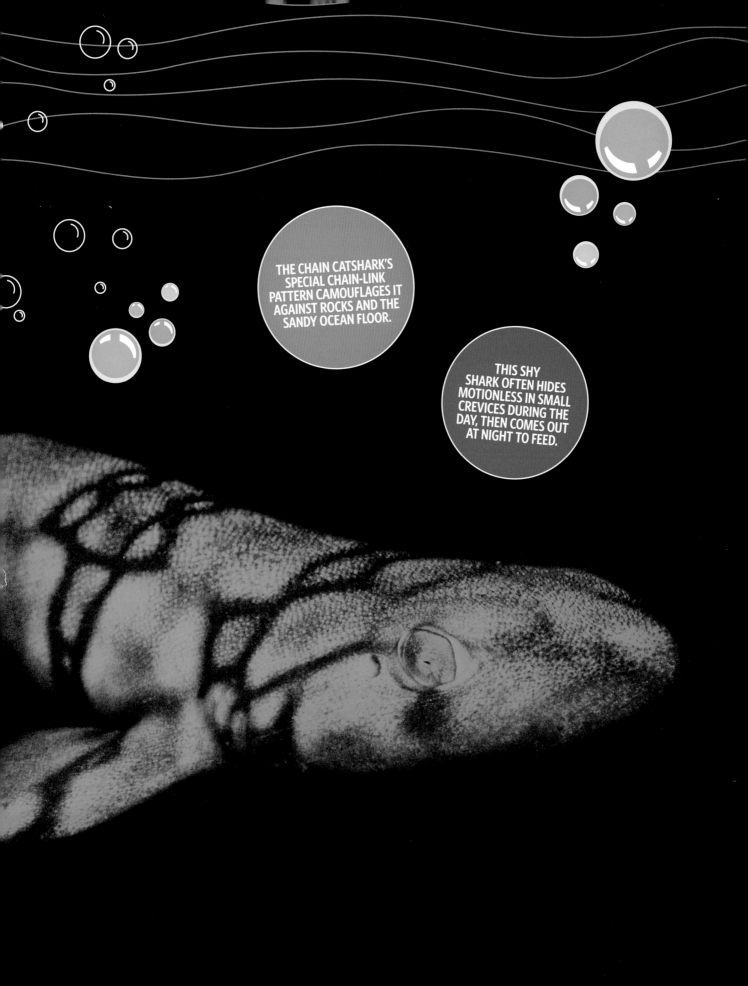

FISH FUNNIES

KNOCK, KNOCK.

Who's there?
Beach.
Beach who?
Bet I'd beach you in a swim race!

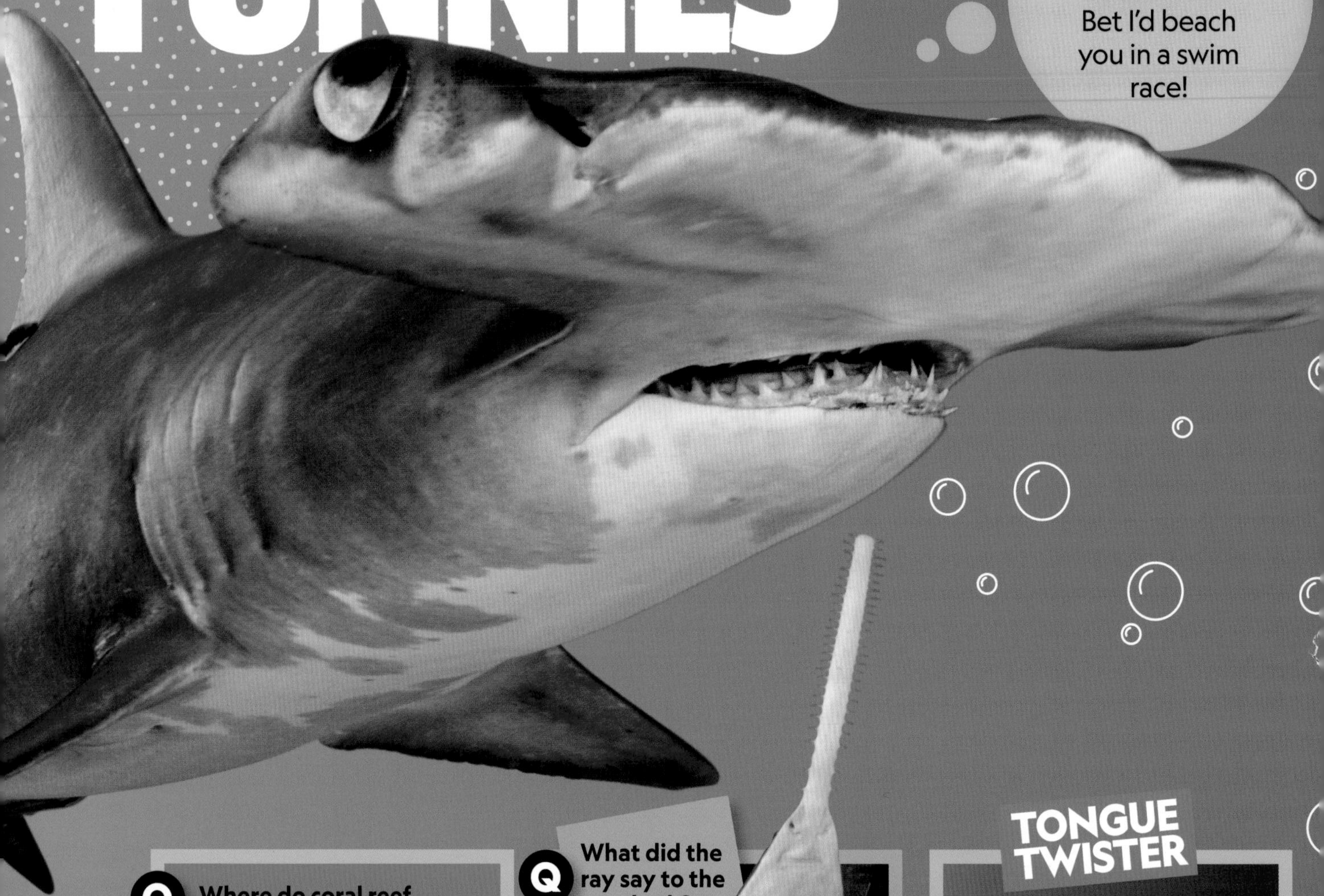

Q **Where do coral reef sharks store their food?**

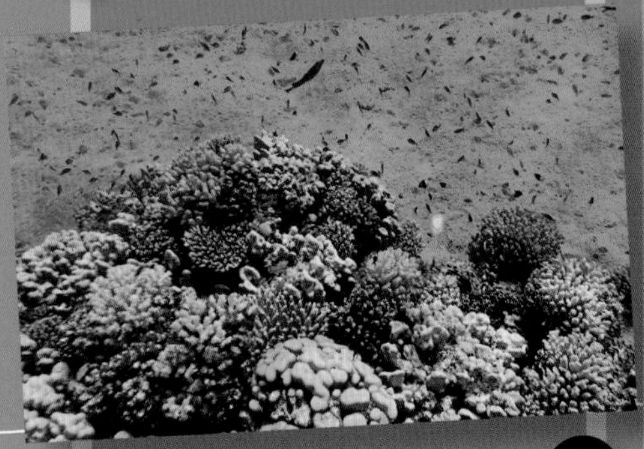

A **In reef-frigerators.**

Q **What did the ray say to the sawshark?**

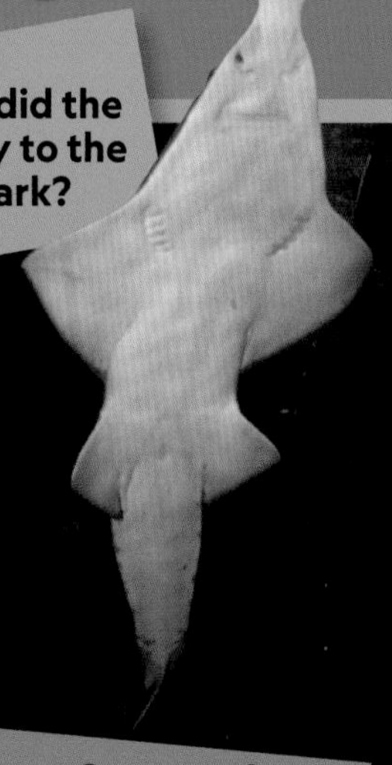

A **"Why the long face?"**

TONGUE TWISTER

SAY THIS FAST THREE TIMES:
The lucky lemon shark licked lots of lollipops.

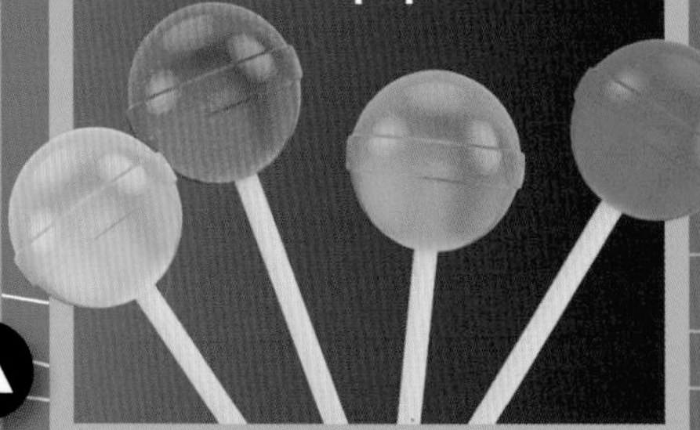

LAUGHABLE *LIST*

A Shark's Chores

Feed the dogfish.

Sweep the seafloor.

Tide-y the bedroom.

Vacuum the carpet shark.

YOU'VE GOT TO BE JOKING ...

Q

What's a shark's favorite number?

A Ate.

RIDDLE ME THIS ...

Q

What are famous sharks called?

A Star fish.

SHARK SUPER-POWERS

Bonnethead sharks have a special fluid in their bodies that lets them know when another bonnethead is nearby.

Instead of sleeping, sharks have resting periods throughout the day with their eyes open **so they can still sense their surroundings.**

SHARKS DON'T HAVE **TYPICAL PAIN RECEPTORS** IN THEIR BRAINS LIKE HUMANS, SO THEY MAY OFTEN BATTLE WITH PREY OR PREDATORS WITHOUT FEELING IT.

Researchers believe **stingray venom** doesn't bother great hammerheads, because stingray barbs are often found in their mouths.

By taking a gulp of air above the surface, **sand tiger sharks** can float enough to approach their prey virtually motionless.

TWO-THIRDS OF THE TOTAL WEIGHT OF A **SHARK'S BRAIN IS** DEDICATED TO ITS SENSE OF SMELL.

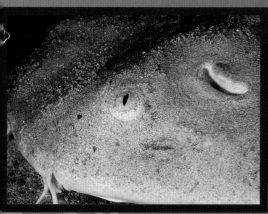

Some sharks, like angel sharks, have **tiny gill slits** behind their eyes that help them breathe when their body is **hiding under sand.**

Sound travels farther and faster underwater, making sound often the first thing a shark senses about prey.

AUSTRALIAN SWELL SHARKS ARE ABLE TO SURVIVE FOR MORE THAN A DAY OUT OF WATER.

Turn the page for more facts about amazing shark superpowers!

Bright white teeth **might help camouflage** the **frilled shark's** dull brown body, **luring in prey** that mistake its teeth for food.

THE **AMERICAN POCKET SHARK** RELEASES A GLOWING GOO SO BRIGHT THAT PREY DON'T NOTICE THE SHARK, AND THEN THE SHARK ATTACKS.

Glasses help **human eyes** create sharper images, but **lamnid sharks** warm muscles behind their eyes to help make images clearer as needed.

While most sharks have to stay in the ocean to survive, **bull sharks** are one of the few sharks that can **travel into rivers.**

THE SILKY SHARK HAS A STRONG SENSE OF HEARING, WHICH HELPS IT LOCATE PREY INCLUDING TUNA, CRAB, AND SQUID.

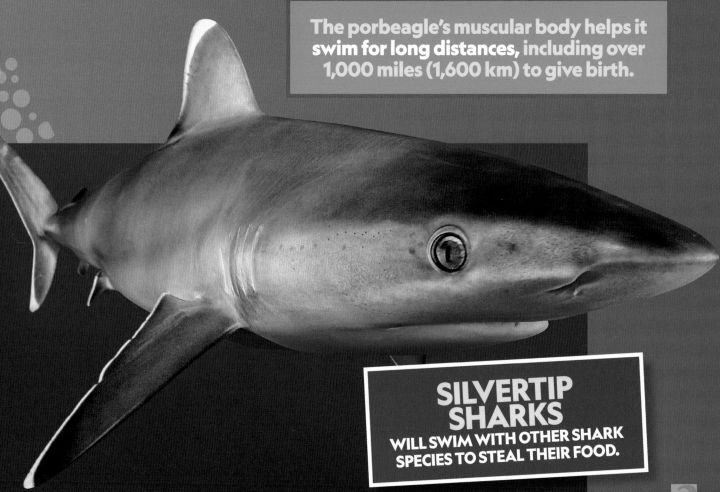

The porbeagle's muscular body helps it swim for long distances, including over 1,000 miles (1,600 km) to give birth.

SILVERTIP SHARKS WILL SWIM WITH OTHER SHARK SPECIES TO STEAL THEIR FOOD.

SHARK LOLs

KNOCK, KNOCK.

Who's there?
Dorsal.
Dorsal who?
Open the dorsal
I can see you!

Q Why was the shark feeling funny?

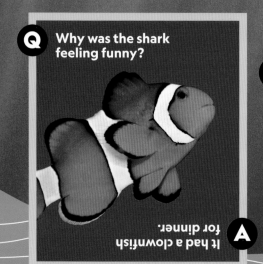

A It had a clownfish for dinner.

Q Why does everyone like the honeycomb catshark?

A Because it's so sweet.

RIDDLE ME THIS ...

Q

Found in a shark's home, these can be big and strong but take lots of breaks.

A Ocean waves.

MEGAMOUTH SHARK: I wonder why no one trusts me with secrets.

ANGEL SHARK: Well, you're kind of a bigmouth.

YOU'VE GOT TO BE JOKING ...

Q

Who delivers presents to sharks on Christmas?

A Santa Jaws.

UP CLOSE AND PERSONAL

Talk about a close encounter with sharks! These zoomed-in photos feature shark parts and other things found in a shark's world. Can you figure out what's shown in each picture? (Hint: Check out the drawing of a shark body on pages 12–13 for clues.) Write down your guesses on a separate piece of paper. Then compare them to the answer key at the bottom of page 95. Game on!

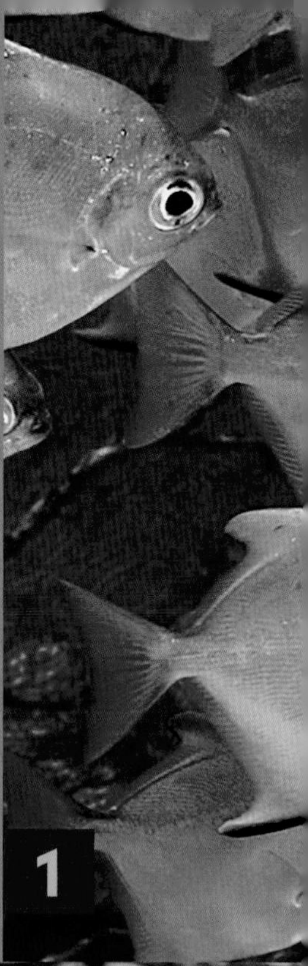

1

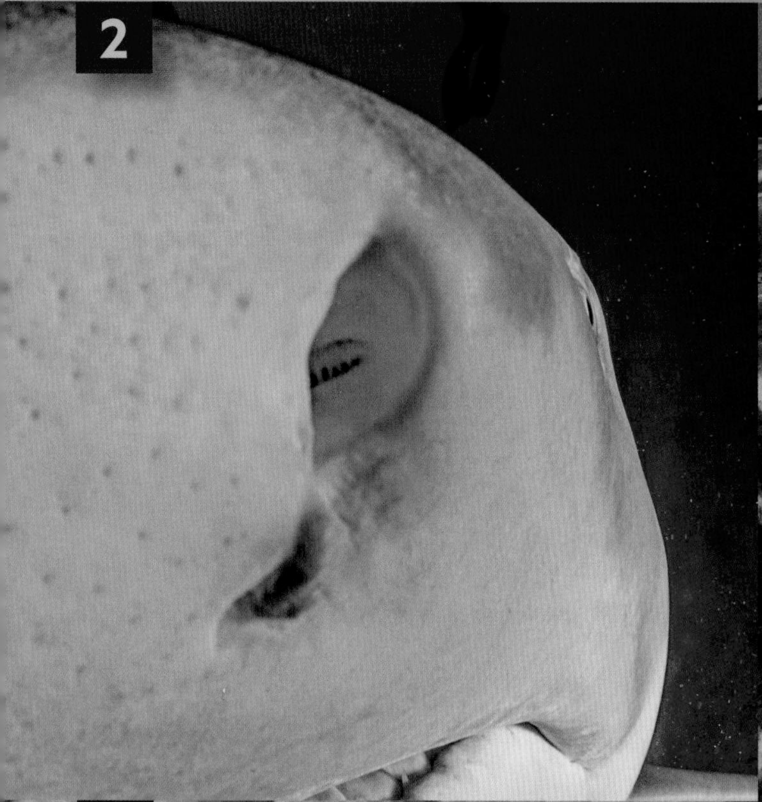

2

3

4

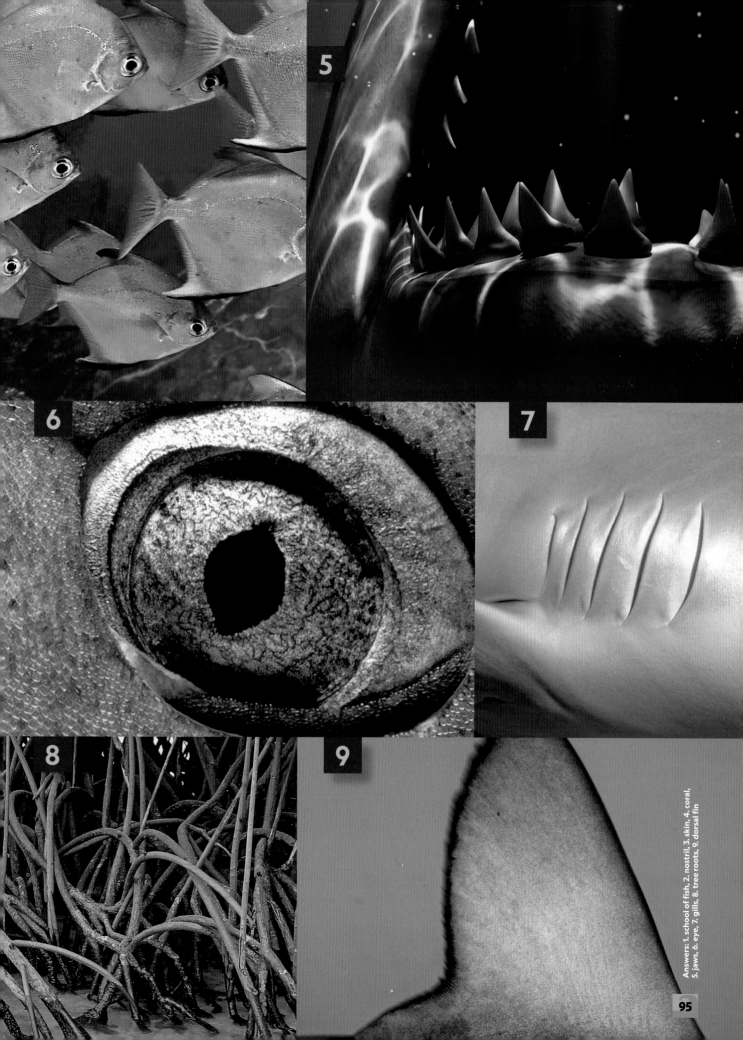

5

6

7

8

9

A HAMMERHEAD'S FAVORITE MEAL

GRACE CASSELBERRY, MARINE SCIENTIST

I use electronic tags to track great hammerheads and Atlantic tarpon—a large silver fish and one of the shark's favorite meals—throughout the ocean. Tarpon come from across the southeastern United States to the Florida Keys before they lay their eggs each spring. One thing I wanted to learn was if the same hammerheads would return year after year to these tarpon gathering sites to feed.

REEL SUSPENSE

On the first day of my second year of tagging, my team and I were excited to find out if we would see any of last year's sharks as we explored the Keys. All of a sudden, a school of fish came tearing past our boat, followed by the tall dorsal fin of a great hammerhead shark. Quickly, I threw a fishing line into the water to try to catch the shark. The hammerhead came up toward the surface and started to home in on the bait. Great hammerheads are incredibly quick and athletic. It is amazing to watch their dorsal fin cut through the water as they quickly switch directions. The shark grabbed the bait, and just as the line started to rip through my hands, I pulled back against the swimming shark. Then it was hooked—our first great hammerhead of the season!

SUCCESS!

When we got the shark to the side of the boat, I realized that I'd seen this shark before. I had tagged her the prior year, and now she was back to feed on the tarpon schools again. I measured her to see how much she had grown and gave her a new tag to track her movements for the next year. It is rare to get to tag the same shark twice, and it was incredible to watch her swim away from our boat a second time.

Hammerhead seen during the study

Grace and her team prepare to release a great hammerhead shark after tagging. The tag will let her track where the shark swims for up to 10 years after it is released!

SUPER-SPEEDY SHARKS

You can't call these sharks slowpokes. The fish usually cruise along at a relaxed pace. But for short bursts, they can torpedo through the water at top speed! The fish crank up their speed to chase prey. Check out just how fast some sharks can swim.

BLUE SHARK
24.5 mph
(39.4 km/h)

GREAT WHITE SHARK
35 mph
(56 km/h)

FINISH

THE REGULAR SWIMMING SPEED OF MOST SHARKS IS ABOUT 1.5 MILES AN HOUR (2.4 KM/H).

BULL SHARK
11 mph
(19 km/h)

TIGER SHARK
20 mph
(32 km/h)

EAT MY BUBBLES!

SHORTFIN MAKO SHARK
46 mph
(74 km/h)

1st

MEET MEGALODON!

A GIANT BEAST GLIDES THROUGH THE OCEAN.

It's ready to chomp down on anything in its path. When it spots a small whale, it charges forward. Catching up to its prey, the creature opens its huge jaws and gobbles up the snack. This isn't some mythical sea monster with a big appetite. It's a megalodon (MEH-gah-LO-don), a type of shark that existed from around 20 to 3.6 million years ago.

SUPERSIZE SHARK

Megalodon is the largest shark known to have ever existed. It was as long as a bus! Its teeth could be seven inches (18 cm) long—about the length of a stapler. And when open, its jaws were up to 11 feet (3.4 m) wide—that's a little wider than an average one-car garage door. What's more, the jaws were super strong. A megalodon's bite could have crushed an automobile. Yikes!

A BIG DISCOVERY

How do we know so much about megalodon? Scientists have found teeth left behind by the sharks. By studying them, they were able to figure out the shark's overall size. Based on where the teeth were found, they also determined that the sharks lived in warm waters all over the world. What's more, the scientists found ancient whale bones with bite marks that may have come from megalodon. This gave scientists hints about the diet of this supersize fish. Scientists are still searching for clues to learn even more. Whatever else they find, one thing's for sure: Megalodon is a really big deal!

THE WORD "MEGALODON" MEANS "GIANT TOOTH" IN GREEK.

MEGALODON MAY HAVE EATEN 2,500 POUNDS (1,130 KG) OF FOOD A DAY.

FISH
FUNNIES

KNOCK, KNOCK.

Who's there?
Sawsharks.
Sawsharks who?
I saw sharks today, and they looked really cool.

Q What's a shark's favorite country?

A Finland.

Q What kind of card games do sharks play?

A Go Fish.

TONGUE TWISTER

SAY THIS FAST THREE TIMES:
Sharks swallow shredded seagrass.

SHARK 1: What's your costume for Halloween?

SHARK 2: I'm going as a Great Fright Shark!

YOU'VE GOT TO BE JOKING ...

Q Why was the shark singing and laughing?

A It was feeling jaw-lly.

KNOCK, KNOCK.

Who's there?
Gill.
Gill who?
Gill you come and hang out with me?

SUPER SHARK TECHNOLOGY

An **app and online map** lets everyone around the world observe and track hundreds of **tagged sharks** and **marine animals.**

Cutting-edge drones soar over the ocean to capture images of where sharks gather and why.

The **WasteShark** is a drone that keeps sharks and sea life healthy by collecting up to **33,000 pounds** (15,000 kg) of plastic and debris a year.

Anyone can join in on the fun of tracking whale sharks by taking a picture of a shark's side and uploading it to the "Wildbook for Whale Sharks."

SCIENTISTS CREATED A
SHARK-EYE CAMERA
THAT SHOWS HOW SHARKS SEE EACH OTHER.

Sharks need **salt to survive,** but with salt levels lowering as global temperatures rise, scientists study prehistoric shark teeth for clues to how sharks might adjust.

Doctors use a **patch made with shark cartilage** to treat third-degree burns and help with **regrowing skin tissue.**

FOSSIL FINDS

Sharks have been around for hundreds of millions of years. The sharks that lived long ago are different from today's sharks. Scientists have found fossils of ancient sharks around the world. Check out some of the coolest finds and the curious clues they give us about these creatures.

What: *Helicoprion*
Where: Idaho, U.S.A.
How Old: 270 million years
Cool Clues: *Helicoprion* sported a spiral-shaped jaw covered in teeth. Scientists think the fish could move its jaw like a buzz saw!

NORTH AMERICA

Idaho, U.S.A.

Kansas, U.S.A.

Illinois, U.S.A.

ATLANTIC OCEAN

What: *Bandringa*
Where: Illinois, U.S.A.
How Old: 307 million years
Cool Clues: Scientists found fossils of baby *Bandringa* sharks in northeastern Illinois—evidence of an ancient shark nursery. These river dwellers had long, Pinocchio-like noses that they likely used to dig for food in riverbeds.

Peru

SOUTH AMERICA

PACIFIC OCEAN

HOW DID FOSSILS OF SHARKS GET ON LAND? OFTENTIMES, LAND WITH SHARK FOSSILS WAS ONCE COVERED IN WATER. ANCIENT SHARK TEETH HAVE ALSO WASHED UP ON LAND FROM THE SEA.

What: *Carcharodon hubbelli*
Where: Peru
How Old: 4.5 million years
Cool Clues: This fossil includes part of the skull of an ancient white shark. It reveals that all white sharks likely came from a family of sharks known as broad-toothed makos.

What: *Cretoxyrhina mantelli*

Where: Kansas, U.S.A.

How Old: 85 million years

Cool Clues: One fossil of an ancient flying reptile called a pterosaur was found with a shark tooth in it. It's possible the fish had leaped from the sea to chomp on the reptile!

What: *Asteracanthus verrucosus*

Where: England, U.K.

How Old: 142 million years

Cool Clues: This ancient shark was covered in spines. If attacked, it would raise its spines, making it more difficult for predators to catch and swallow.

England, U.K.

EUROPE

Morocco

ASIA

AFRICA

PACIFIC OCEAN

INDIAN OCEAN

Australia

0   2,000 mi
0   2,000 km

What: *Carcharocles angustidens*

Where: Australia

How Old: 25 million years

Cool Clues: The teeth from this shark are 2.8 inches (7 cm) long. The fish must have had a big mouth to fit these huge pearly whites. In fact, scientists think it was twice as big as a great white's!

SOUTHERN OCEAN

ANTARCTICA

What: *Phoebodus*

Where: Morocco

How Old: At least 360 million years

Cool Clues: This shark's chompers faced inward. This suggests that the fish used its teeth to nab prey and then swallowed it whole—no chewing required.

BABY SHARKS

COOLEST SKIN PATTERNS

TIGER SHARK

Tiger sharks in Hawaii, U.S.A., give birth when the beautiful wiliwili trees blossom, which means it's autumn in Hawaii. Though tiger sharks are one of the top predators on the planet, their feline name also stems from their babies. When a tiger shark is born it has more defined "tiger stripes," but as the tiger shark gets older, these lines fade away, turning more into dots and dashes.

BIGGEST FAMILY FEUD

SAND TIGER SHARK

Sand tiger sharks live up to their fearsome feline namesake before they are even born. They begin to battle their siblings in the womb, often eating each other, until there is only one survivor. There can be around 100 babies inside a sand tiger mother at once. Some babies develop faster and bigger than their siblings, and so begins their smaller sibling feeding spree.

SHARPEST SENSES

BAMBOO SHARK

While still in their eggs, baby bamboo sharks can sense odors, water flow, and electrical fields made by large fish and other shark predators. Baby bamboo shark senses are so developed that scientists study them to learn how to make a shark repellent that could help keep sharks away from surfers.

MOST-SWALLOWED BABY TEETH

GREAT WHITE SHARK

Unlike humans, baby sharks, including baby great whites, are born with a full set of teeth. Great white pups will even shed teeth in the womb, likely swallowing them for extra calcium and nutrients. They need to be as strong as they can: When great whites are born, they swim away from their mother, already able to take care of themselves.

SHOCKING SHARK FACTS

A whale shark's mouth **is** five feet (1.5 m) across, **which is nearly as wide as the length of a bicycle.**

WATER FLOWS THROUGH SHARK SCALES WITHOUT MAKING ANY SOUND, SO A SHARK CAN **SILENTLY STALK PREY.**

Some sharks will have a **belly button** for a few months after giving birth to live young.

Sharks have been known to eat all sorts of **strange things—snakes, birds,** even **polar bears** and **porcupines!**

SOMETIMES SHARKS ARE REFERRED TO AS **"SWIMMING NOSES"** BECAUSE THEIR SENSE OF SMELL IS THEIR MOST POWERFUL WEAPON.

The draughtsboard shark is known for **barking** like a dog.

Sharks can't **sneeze.** If something gets in one of their nostrils, they have to **shake it out.**

Sharks don't use their **nostrils** for breathing—just smelling!

THE **EPAULETTE SHARK** IS ONE OF THE FEW SHARKS THAT CAN USE ITS FINS TO "WALK"—THROUGH CREVICES, ALONG THE OCEAN FLOOR, AND EVEN ON LAND AT LOW TIDE!

PLANET PROTECTORS

HOW DO SHARKS FIGHT FOR OUR PLANET?

Sharks might not wear capes or have magical powers. But when it comes to helping the Earth, they're true superheroes. Sharks are known as apex predators. That means they are at the "top" of the food web and have few natural predators. As the head honchos of their habitats, these fish play a critical role.

CARING FOR CORAL

Sharks are important to coral reefs. Sharks that live along these reefs feed on smaller predators such as grouper fish. The smaller predators munch on plant-eating fish. And the plant-eating fish eat algae off coral. If sharks disappeared, the population of the smaller predators would increase. They would eat more plant-eating fish. And without these plant-eaters, too much algae would grow on coral, damaging it.

SAVING OUR SUPERHEROES

We need to protect sharks so they can continue to protect Earth! Sharks face threats from pollution and overfishing. One way to help is for countries to turn nearby waters into shark sanctuaries (SANK-chu-AIR-ees), or official safe spots, where people are not allowed to fish for sharks. As of 2021, 17 of these exist around the world. Hopefully, there will be more to come. Want to help save sharks? Write letters to local and national officials asking them to keep sharks safe!

CARIBBEAN REEF SHARKS, GRAY REEF SHARKS, BLACKTIPS, WHITETIPS, AND SILVERTIPS ARE ALL SPECIES THAT LIVE AROUND CORAL REEFS.

SAVING SEAGRASS

Coral isn't the only thing sharks protect. These finned bodyguards also keep seagrass safe. Animals that eat this grass, such as sea turtles, are afraid of sharks. So, they move around a lot as they feed to avoid the fish. With no sharks around, the sea turtles would gobble up the best patches of grass until they were gone. That would be bad for critters living in the seagrass, like shellfish.

KEEPING IT COOL

By guarding seagrass, sharks also fight climate change! Seagrass absorbs a gas called carbon dioxide (DIE-OX-ide) from the atmosphere. This gas gets stored in the plants and seabed. If too many animals disturb the seagrass, the gas may get released. And once the gas goes back into the atmosphere, it warms the planet. Sharks keep the number of animals around seagrass down. That means they protect the grass, and this helps slow climate change. Sharks are real-life heroes, and they're here to save the day!

SHARK LOLs

Q What did the dentist say to the shark?

A "Please don't open wide!"

Q What does a hammer-head shark say when it does a good job?

A "I nailed it!"

A It was in a sour mood.

CATSHARK 1: Boo!

CATSHARK 2: Eeek! Don't sneak up on me!

CATSHARK 1: You're a real scaredy-catshark.

RIDDLE ME THIS ...

Q A shark needs them to survive but is always losing them. What are they?

A Teeth.

TONGUE TWISTER

SAY THIS FAST THREE TIMES:
Fish swim through the salty seas.

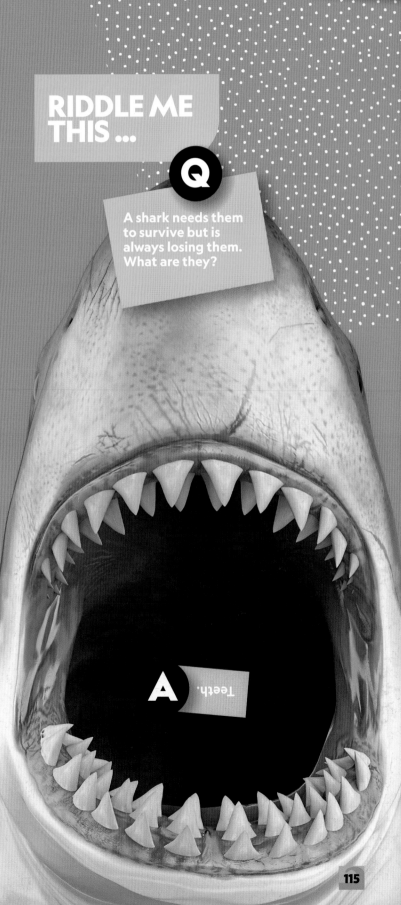

BATTLE OF THE SHARK PATTERNS

Sharks come in many different shapes, sizes, and patterns! Who knew sharks aren't all gray or blue? Here's a fun scratch-and-reveal craft to help you compare the many different amazing and wacky shark skin patterns.

YOU WILL NEED:
DISH SOAP
ACRYLIC PAINT (color of your choice)
PAINTBRUSH
A SHEET OF DRAWING PAPER
CLEAR PACKING TAPE
COLORED PENCILS, MARKERS, OR CRAYONS
(OPTIONAL: GREEN HIGHLIGHTER)

STEP 1:
With a pencil, divide the paper into four equal-size sections.

STEP 2:
Draw a different shark pattern in each of the four sections. Use the examples and your colored pencils, markers, or crayons to draw or trace one pattern onto each of your four sections.

WHALE SHARK (pages 82–83)

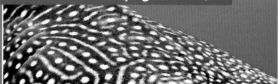

WOBBEGONG (pages 54–55)

CHAIN CATSHARK (pages 84–85)

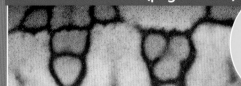

CONSIDER USING A GREEN HIGH-LIGHTER TO SHOW THEIR GLOW!

TIGER SHARK (page 99)

STEP 3:

Cover the front and back of the paper with tape to laminate. (If you need to cut off excess tape around the edges, ask an adult for help first.)

STEP 4:

Mix two parts paint with one part soap.

STEP 5:

Paint over the laminated paper. You may need to do a few layers to make sure the patterns underneath are not visible—let it dry for a few minutes between layers.

STEP 6:

When the paint is dry, it's time to scratch away! Draw the outline of your favorite shark shapes or an awesome shark scene on the paper. Scratch inside of your lines to reveal the cool shark patterns! To see these sharks in action, look at the pages noted in step 2.

STEP 7:

See how many other shark patterns and cool camouflage colors you can find throughout the book to make even more pattern battles!

NURSE SHARKS

ARE KNOWN TO REST IN GROUPS OF 40,

PILING ON TOP OF

ONE ANOTHER.

THEY ALSO HOVER OVER THE OCEAN FLOOR—RESTING ON THEIR PECTORAL FINS—TO CREATE A FALSE CAVE THAT LURES IN CRABS AND LOBSTERS.

QUIZ TIME

1 How long can Australian swell sharks survive out of water?

a. more than an hour

b. more than a day

c. more than a month

d. more than a year

2 How wide is a whale shark's mouth?

a. as wide as a plate

b. as wide as a car

c. as wide as a bicycle

d. as wide as a carousel

3 A spinner shark can jump _____ out of the water.

a. five feet (1.5 m)

b. 10 feet (3 m)

c. 15 feet (4.6 m)

d. 20 feet (6 m)

4 True or false: Some sharks can grow 20,000 teeth during their lives.

a. true

b. false

5 Which shark walks along the seafloor on its fins?

a. the epaulette shark

b. the fins-for-hands shark

c. the silvertip shark

d. the basking shark

6 How much food did megalodon probably eat in a day?

a. 600 pounds (270 kg)

b. 1,200 pounds (540 kg)

c. 2,500 pounds (1,130 kg)

d. 3,000 pounds (1,360 kg)

7 Which shark barks like a dog?

   a. the blue shark

   b the megamouth shark

   c. the bull shark

   d. the draughtsboard shark

8 Shark scales are made of a material similar to a human's _____.

   a. tooth enamel

   b. fingernails

   c. nose hairs

   d. earlobes

9 Which shark gulps water to grow bigger when threatened?

   a. the Caribbean reef shark

   b. the bluntnose sixgill shark

   c. the swell shark

   d. the megamouth shark

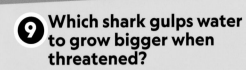

10 How much of a shark's brain is devoted to smell?

   a. one-third

   b. one-half

   c. two-thirds

   d. the whole brain

11 Which shark has the most toxic bite?

   a. the puffadder shyshark

   b. the dwarf lanternshark

   c. the viper dogfish shark

   d. the horn shark

12 How fast can a great white shark swim?

   a. 35 miles an hour (56 km/h)

   b. 30 miles an hour (48 km/h)

   c. 25 miles an hour (40 km/h)

   d. 11 miles an hour (18 km/h)

FIND OUT MORE

Want to dive even deeper into the world of sharks? Check out these books, and ask a grown-up to help you learn more about these amazing explorers.

BOOKS

Beneath the Waves: Celebrating the Ocean Through Pictures, Poems, and Stories by Stephanie Warren Drimmer. National Geographic Kids, 2020.

Citizens of the Sea: Wondrous Creatures From the Census of Marine Life by Nancy Knowlton. National Geographic, 2010.

Everything Sharks by Ruth A. Musgrave. National Geographic Kids, 2011.

Face to Face With Sharks by David Doubilet and Jennifer Hayes. National Geographic, 2009.

Mission: Shark Rescue: All About Sharks and How to Save Them by Ruth A. Musgrave. National Geographic Kids, 2016.

Sharks! Sticker Activity Book: Over 1,000 Stickers! National Geographic Kids, 2014.

The Ultimate Book of Sharks by Brian Skerry, with Elizabeth Carney and Sarah Wassner Flynn. National Geographic Kids, 2018.

Ultimate Oceanpedia: The Most Complete Ocean Reference Ever by Christina Wilsdon. National Geographic Kids, 2016.

Caribbean reef shark

EXPLORERS

An explorer is someone who takes their work out into the field to learn more about it. They research questions, make observations, and report what they discover.

Tsiory Andrianavalona, paleontologist and researcher

Grace Casselberry, marine scientist

Naomi Clark-Shen, marine biologist, conservationist, and researcher

Jess Cramp, shark researcher, ecologist, diver, and marine conservationist

Austin Gallagher, marine biologist, ecologist, diver, and conservationist

Lucy A. Hawkes, biologist, physiological ecologist, and animal tracking expert

Yannis Papastamatiou, diver, educator, researcher, and marine biologist

Brian Skerry, photojournalist, diver, conservationist, and author

Daniela Vilema, journalist, educator, and environmental communicator

Great white shark

Tiger shark pup

INDEX

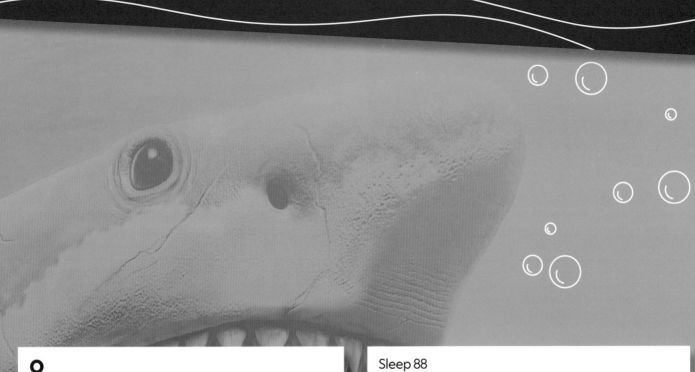

CREDITS

ACKNOWLEDGMENTS

NATIONAL GEOGRAPHIC and Yellow Border Design are trademarks of the National Geographic Society, used under license.

Since 1888, the National Geographic Society has funded more than 14,000 research, conservation, education, and storytelling projects around the world. National Geographic Partners distributes a portion of the funds it receives from your purchase to National Geographic Society to support programs including the conservation of animals and their habitats. To learn more, visit natgeo.com/info.

For more information, visit nationalgeographic.com, call 1-877-873-6846, or write to the following address:

National Geographic Partners, LLC
1145 17th Street N.W.
Washington, DC 20036-4688 U.S.A.

For librarians and teachers:
nationalgeographic.com/books/librarians-and-educators

More for kids from National Geographic: natgeokids.com

National Geographic Kids magazine inspires children to explore their world with fun yet educational articles on animals, science, nature, and more. Using fresh story-telling and amazing photography, *Nat Geo Kids* shows kids ages 6 to 14 the fascinating truth about the world—and why they should care. **natgeo.com/subscribe**

For rights or permissions inquiries, please contact National Geographic Books Subsidiary Rights: bookrights@natgeo.com

Designed by Eva Absher-Schantz and Julide Dengel

Library of Congress Cataloging-in-Publication Data

Names: Silen, Andrea, author. I Hargrave, Kelly, author.
Title: Can't get enough shark stuff : fun facts, awesome info, cool games, silly jokes, and more! / by Andrea Silen and Kelly Hargrave.
Description: Washington, DC : National Geographic, 2022. I Series: Can't get enough I Includes bibliographical references and index. I Audience: Ages 7-10 I Audience: Grades 2-3
Identifiers: LCCN 2021011922 I ISBN 9781426372582 (paperback) I ISBN 9781426372599 (library binding)
Subjects: LCSH: Sharks--Juvenile literature.
Classification: LCC QL638.9 .S545 2022 I DDC 597.3--dc23
LC record available at https://lccn.loc.gov/2021011922

The publisher would like to acknowledge the following people for making this book possible: Andrea Silen and Kelly Hargrave, writers; Jen Agresta, project editor; Eva Absher-Schantz, VP, visual identity and art director; Julide Dengel, art director; Sarah J. Mock, senior photo editor; Michaela Weglinski and Avery Naughton, assistant editors; Michelle Harris, fact-checker; Alix Inchausti, production editor; and Anne LeongSon and Gus Tello, design production assistants.

Printed in China
21/PPS/1